GOD, PRAYER, AND HEALING

God, Prayer, and Healing

Living with God in a World Like Ours

ARTHUR A. VOGEL

WILLIAM B. EERDMANS PUBLISHING COMPANY
GRAND RAPIDS, MICHIGAN

© 1995 Wm. B. Eerdmans Publishing Co.

255 Jefferson Ave. S.E., Grand Rapids, Michigan 49503

Printed in the United States of America

00 99 98 97 96 95   7 6 5 4 3 2 1

Library of Congress Cataloging-in-Publication Data

Vogel, Arthur Anton.
God, prayer, and healing: living with God in a world like ours /
Arthur A. Vogel.
p.   cm.
ISBN 0-8028-0786-0 (pbk.)
1. Christian life. 2. God — Knowableness. 3. Prayer — Christianity.
4. Healing — Religious aspects. 5. Self-Knowledge, Theory of.
I. Title.
BV4501.2.V557   1995
248.4 — dc20   94-41456
                                                    CIP

Unless otherwise noted, the Scripture quotations in this publication are from the New Revised Standard Version Bible, copyright © 1989 by the Division of Christian Education of the National Council of Churches of Christ in the U.S.A., and used by permission.

To all who prayed for Tony —
and for those who wonder about praying

Contents

1

*The Problem and
the Problems*

THIS BOOK, although it ranges broadly in its full development,
is not undertaken as an academic treatise on the co-existence of
God, good, and evil. It is not undertaken as a theoretical exercise
and for no other reason than intellectual curiosity. It is undertaken
to witness, after the fact, to the propriety of the faith and hope
lived by our family during the months of the critical illness of
one of our sons.

At the same time, this book, as it has turned out, is not typical
of the testimonies one normally finds witnessing to spiritual
healing and to the presence of God in difficult and threatening
circumstances. The book is too theological for that.

It may pay us to take a moment to consider the last statement, for it may be asked how it is possible for a book — or
for someone, for that matter — to be too theological. Theology
is about God, and, if God exists, it is hard to see how a creature
could be too concerned with the source of creation. As the
creator and sustainer of all that is, God is the beginning and
end of all reality; it is difficult to conceive how too much
attention could be paid to such a one. That being the case, if it
is possible to be too concerned about God, the "too" must refer

to the manner of our concern rather than to the object of our concern.

Taking that point, we can understand how a person or a book can be too theological. Theology is an intellectual exercise; it is a way of thinking and speaking about God by means of abstract concepts and ideas. However, the living God, the only God who is the real God is not an abstract idea. So it is that a person can be too theological if he or she allows abstract thoughts about God either to replace or to allow no time for a fully personal relation with the living God.

We are born into a world of action and activity, and it is only in this world that we are our full selves. Reflection requires a certain withdrawal from the world, for when we reflect upon something, we carry on a conversation with ourselves about it. When we consider the meaning of life or of anything that happens in our lives or in the world, we ask ourselves questions about it. We consider an event from different points of view. But in order to do that, we have to step back from the event and separate ourselves from it; we cannot be totally immersed in it.

Reflection is possible only by distancing ourselves from what we are reflecting upon. It is after we have done something — made a cutting remark that silenced an opponent — or before we have done something — decided whether or not we'll stand up to a bigot — that we reflect upon our action by stepping back from it and observing it as if we were its spectator instead of its agent. It is not difficult to step back from our past lives with God and objectively examine them, and, because the future is not yet, we are sufficiently separated from it to consider how we wish to live with God in time yet to come. But is it possible to step back from God in any significant way in order to make him the object of our thought in the present? There have been yes and no answers to that question in the religious history of humankind, and I will have something to say about it myself, but for all the different ways that knowledge of God has been claimed, no one denies that abstract knowledge about God is less than the living personal relationship with God to which we are called.

In reflective thinking we carry on a dialogue with ourselves about a reality beyond the conversation we are having within ourselves. Thinking about God — theology — is such a conversation, and if our conversation with ourselves about God keeps us from being with God, then we are being too theological. But the reality that theology discusses is also something we live in the fullness of our lives; in fact, the living comes before the discussion. It is from the nature of the living that the discussion is derived. Believers do not just live with God; they live with other people — some of whom are believers and some of whom are not — with God. Not only do we ask questions of ourselves about the world and about our lives in the world; other people ask questions of us about ourselves and about the world. In the end, we cannot help asking ourselves the questions other people ask us about God.

Human life has been described as the quest for meaning, and it is true that when the meaning of our lives is threatened, our lives themselves are threatened. God, the source of life, is the source of meaning, and when the meaning of human life is negated or contradicted in the world, we would be less than human if we did not, as others do, question the existence of God or of God's nature or of God's power. We must reflect upon the meaning of our lives if we are to live meaningful lives in our relation with each other in the world.

God was never more intensely the object of our family's life than during the illness of our son, yet, in all the events that occurred in the hospital in which our son was being treated, it was never more obvious that God is not an object. God's action cannot be predicted, yet God is our comforter and our advocate. Can we live meaningfully with such a God? Can we help reflecting on such tension and mystery in our lives? Others question our belief in God; can we help questioning it ourselves?

Reality is never derived; it is given. Thus reflection cannot replace living. In reflective thinking, we separate ourselves from ourselves, playing the role of other people to ourselves, so that a true internal conversation takes place within us. When our name is called by someone or something beyond us, however, the internal dialogue we have with ourselves is interrupted, and we are recalled to a oneness and unity of being — to the reality of our lives — that thought and reflection alone can never provide. Our name can be called by a friend, an enemy, an impersonal accident, or by God, but when we are called back to ourselves by reality beyond us, our lives are different after reflection than they were before reflection. The activity of our lives is more than our thinking, but we are not our whole selves until our lives are thoughtful.

So it is that action leads to thought and thought supplies meaning to action. When we use all our energy to stand up for what is right, to fight an illness, or to pray to God, we are our unified, whole selves in the activity. Reflection is impossible at those times, for they are times of self-commitment through action; but such activities, being human, are meaningful activities — and we would be less than human if we were not concerned about the meaning in itself. After prayer or before prayer, we would be less than ourselves if we did not consider what we are doing when we pray and ask ourselves such questions as what prayer is, to whom we pray, how we should pray, and whether or not prayer can accomplish anything.

Prayer itself is different after such reflection, and so it is that we offer these reflections about God, prayer, and healing from our ongoing lives with God to our ongoing lives with God.

❧   ❧

When he was thirty-seven years old, our second son discovered some swollen glands in his neck. Testing revealed that Tony had small-celled lymphatic cancer. That cancer is slow growing compared with Hodgkin's disease, and the information we received was encouraging until we learned that the success rate of treatment was much higher for the virulent strain than the indolent strain.

Not quite two weeks after his first chemotherapy treatment, Tony was in his backyard digging fence-post holes. He suddenly became so weak and feverish that, after a short period of lying down in the house, he went to the hospital. The next day he was still complaining of abdominal pain, and his high fever continued. Then he went into septic shock: his heart rate was over 190 beats a minute; he had practically no detectable blood pressure, and his white blood-cell count (normally five to ten thousand) was three hundred.

After emergency surgery that was completed at three in the morning, it was discovered that clostridium, a powerful bacterium that thrives in areas without oxygen, had entered Tony's body through a perforated intestine and was running rampant. Tony's right pectoral muscle had been completely destroyed, and discoloration of the skin indicated that the sepsis had spread to Tony's legs, his left arm, and his left chest area. The doctors told us that they did not expect him to live through the afternoon.

To the surprise of his doctors, Tony hung on that afternoon. He did better than that, for he is alive today and working. To get where he is today, however, he spent almost eight weeks in an intensive care unit. During that time he was heavily sedated with Versed, put on dialysis, given an ileostomy and a tracheotomy, and given innumerable blood transfusions.

Subsequently, after spending a week on a surgical recovery floor, Tony was allowed to go home, where he gradually regained his strength. A few weeks after leaving the hospital, he returned to have the ileostomy reversed. Before his chemotherapy began, he had taken the initial steps to get into an experimental protocol at Stanford University, and, when he contacted Stanford again, he was asked to have some lymph-gland tissue harvested for study when his ileostomy was reversed.

The doctors had considerable difficulty locating any glands in the surgical area because they were so small, but several were finally located. When the sample tissue taken was examined both at the hospital and at Stanford, it was found to have no trace of cancer in it. It was clean! Tony can no longer feel the lymph nodes in his neck that were the first indication of the disease, although a CAT scan has revealed that other nodes appear to be slightly enlarged. Several doctors involved in the case were the first to use the word "miracle" to describe our son's recovery. Another doctor referred to instances of spontaneous healing, and still other doctors referred to a number of documented instances in which remission of cancer has attended the treatment of another major illness. There is no doubt that something wonderful has occurred, but there is also no doubt that ambiguities remain.

Ambiguities remain, but, in the midst of them, something significant happened. It is the commingling of ambiguity and clarity, the juxtaposition of predictable regularities and chance events in our lives, that I want to discuss. The human condition embraces the clear and the unclear, and the period of almost two months during which members of our family occupied seats in the ICU waiting room of St. Joseph's Hospital in Milwaukee intensified our awareness of the tensions involved between those poles.

We had all been praying regularly for Tony before the second crisis occurred. When we arrived at the hospital a few hours before his midnight surgery — we lived six hundred miles away — we were admitted to his bedside, where we prayed with him, for him, and over him. I anointed him on several occasions and passed my hands over his body, especially the obviously infected areas, as regularly as I could during his hospitalization. A respiration therapist, who had been attending Tony the night of his first crisis, saw my wife and me in the hall one day and asked if we would mind if he organized a prayer group of hospital personnel to meet with us to pray for Tony. We were grateful, and two days later a group of about fifteen people — a former patient, his family members, some technicians, a cardiologist, and a chaplain — met with us in the chapel for prayer.

As the weeks went on, we and other members of our family were the longest continuing residents of the waiting room. We saw a number of other families come and go, and we saw the same doctors come and go and come again. The families who stayed longer we got to know better, and with those families we would exchange daily inquiries and information. The same terms used to describe Tony's condition were used to describe other patients' conditions, and we listened as other families were told that the same procedures used on Tony would be used on their loved ones. Clergy also came and went frequently. They did not appear as regularly as the doctors did or the hospital chaplain had, but their conversation with family members and family members' conversation among themselves were almost always similar. We heard about prayers that were being offered among relatives and friends for those lying in the room next door, and we heard about prayer chains and intercession groups that were active beyond the families. The concern, the medical terms, and the prayers were often almost the same, but some of the families were told of deaths, while others were told of beginning recoveries.

To get different results from the same components presents a problem. If the practitioners of scientific medicine are using the same resources in the same facility, and if patients and their families are praying to the same God for healing, why are the healing effects so varied from person to person? What is the relation of prayer to healing? Does God act in human affairs? Can God act in human affairs?

My family and I and many other concerned persons prayed for our son. Other families and friends were praying for their sons and daughters, fathers and mothers, other friends and relatives. At the same time, many physical and chemical procedures were applied to the ones being prayed for. What is the relationship of prayer and science in such instances? Did our prayers add anything to the healing process? Was it reasonable for us to pray with an expectancy that Tony really could be — and would be — healed because of our prayers? Are there any objective results of prayer? Perhaps prayer for the sick is no more than a psychological help to those praying. In the midst of the conflicting reports delivered in the waiting room, we continued to pray with hope. Could that hope be genuine?

In spite of the conflicting events unfolding in the ICU and its waiting room, I believe that the hope we expressed in praying was reasonable for us and significant for our son. I continue to pray with expectancy for those who are ill, and I think such prayer is truly beneficial. I want to offer an unequivocal witness to the necessity for and propriety of healing intercessions. I hope to offer strong support for such intercessory prayer, but I do not want the clarity of my support to be purchased at the expense of denying the ambiguities of reality.

The healing ministry is often advocated with a simplicity that makes it unreal. In such instances, certainty of conviction is purchased at the price of denying reality. Clarity, like simplicity, is always achieved by elimination. If we narrow our focus sufficiently, we will finally be able to see one thing clearly, but we must not then pretend that what we clearly see is all there is to reality. That is what appears to happen frequently with "spiritual healing," however. A person's illness is a problem for him or her.

Told to bring that problem to God, the person prays for healing as if nothing existed but the person and God. Told to pray for healing and to expect healing, the person does, and, let us say, the person is healed. The healing is a wonderful confirmation of faith and is taken by the person as proof that God heals in response to prayer. A problem is solved; a witness is made; and the practice of spiritual healing is recommended.

In such a healing, a problem — the illness — has been solved. The problem and its solution can be clearly presented and advocated, but the clarity of the solution depends upon the isolation of the instance. When an individual healing is seen in the context of all those in a given hospital, let alone wider areas of inclusion, what appeared to be a solution in the narrow context presents new problems in the wider context. To isolate ourselves with God and act, on the one hand, as if only he and we exist, and then on the other hand to recommend our relationship with God to others has a certain slippage. The clarity we purchase by isolation turns out to be at best an ambiguity in the wider picture — and in some instances may even present a contradiction. Is it reasonable to "believe and expect" at the individual level, when ambiguity and inconsistency are found at a more inclusive level?

I believe that such belief is reasonable. That reasonableness will be the subject of my discussion, but in that discussion I will not forget those who spent time in the waiting room and who were told that their loved ones, instead of being healed, had died. Their experience is as much the topic of my concern as is Tony's healing.

The relationship of prayer to healing offers something of a paradigm of religious living in the world generally. The polar components we discover in healing are the polar components of our lives in the world at large — the objectivity of science and the subjectivity of personal presence. Science, to be sure, is an activity of persons, but it is an activity of persons studying the world and themselves as objectively as possible. To be objective requires that we treat the world and ourselves as objects. Impartial objectivity and the impersonal repeatability of scientific experiment lie at the foundation of scientific methodology and of the world that technology has built upon that foundation. When a scientist leaves her laboratory, however, she resents being treated as an object. Our intimate, personal lives cannot be contained in abstract equations and mathematical formulae; unvarying predictability, the goal of scientific activity, is the source of boredom over the weekend. Sporting events and other activities in which the outcome is uncertain are what intrigue us. We are most ourselves where we can make — or even watch other people make — a difference in events, where human presence counts.

Prayer and healing involve the subjective-objective polarity I have been describing. It is commonplace to refer to the practice of medicine as both a science and an art: its scientific dimension utilizes objective and repeatable observations that apply to all individuals in exactly the same sense, while its artful dimension takes account of the subjective nature of the patient, the doctor, and their interrelations. In our industrialized and cybernated society, medical activities are often summarily referred to as "the health-care industry." That industry, like every other industry, is concerned with the effective and efficient delivery of its product. It is to that end that illness is considered, and patients themselves are frequently regarded as no more than objects. There has always been some reaction against such practice, but presently the protest is gaining momentum and becoming stronger than ever. The importance of personal relations is increasingly emphasized in medical circles today, and, in that light, prayer should not be excluded from consideration, for it is a personal relationship between a believer and God. Our question is whether or not that personal relationship makes a significant contribution to human health. We know that doctors act. Can God?

The Problem and the Problems

Considering the relationship of prayer to healing involves us in the relationship of prayer to science, or, more adequately put, it brings us to the relationship between meaning in the world of religion — the world in which prayer is reasonable — and meaning in the world of science — the world of objective inquiry. Because we are concerned with human health, we are concerned with the nature of human life. I have faulted the advocacy of prayer and spiritual healing in personalized contexts that are too narrow, so, in beginning this advocacy, I will start with some descriptive remarks about what life in the world is like. If we are concerned with human health in our personal lives, we must start in the recognizable world in which we live as persons. That world contains both predictable and unpredictable events, certainties and uncertainties, subjective and objective elements.

Once we find ourselves in the world, no matter what our personal views and opinions may be, we all share the common task of getting through life. In one way or another we all answer, by our lives, the question, "How are we to get through life?" The three elements of that question — *we, getting through,* and *life* — are my concern here. I will try to suggest what I think is the best combination we can make of them. In doing so, the goal will be to try to discover and be honest about who we are, what life in the world is like, and how we can best get through the world without denying the nature of either ourselves or the world.

I will begin by offering a description of human life in the world. It is important to recognize that, whatever our differences in the end, we all begin in the same place.

2

Life in the World

WHAT is life in the world like? What are the conditions the world sets for our lives? When are we most ourselves? Who are we, and when do we feel we are most fully alive? These are the first questions we must ask.

Novels are about life, and we know the difference between a good and a bad novel. In a good one, we live the story being told. In a poor one, the characters are lifeless. The plot is obviously a premeditated structure into which the characters are forced; it does not offer a meaning that gradually emerges from their decisions.

A good novel involves me, the reader, in the spontaneity of the lives about which I am reading. Living the story with the characters portrayed, I live in the time they live as they live it; I participate in the uncertainties and ambiguities they experience from their points of view. I am taken into their situation; I am not able to abstract myself from their time and know their future with a certainty beyond them.

To abstract formal structures from our lives has been condemned as the work of philosophy, and it has been offered as the reason why philosophic principles make so little difference in our lives. A philosopher, according to Richard Rorty, typically tries to discover a universal nature found in all human beings, but, because such an abstract nature belongs to everyone equally, it makes no special difference to anyone. A poet, on the other hand, is more modest, for the poet, instead of trying to discover what is the same for everyone and to hold up necessary truths, describes the accidental and changing dimensions of our lives. Poets describe the immediate, human world in which we live; they deal with the contingencies of our lives. From the point of view of philosophy, such details are unimportant, but it is the immediate "thickness" of the contingencies we experience, described by poets, that most readily move us to action. Any lover worth his salt knows that a poem will do more on a starlit night than a philosophic treatise on love.

The search for universal natures and absolute certainty leads to platitudes or mathematics, neither of which reveals to anyone who he or she really is. Our lives do not unfold in an uninterrupted logical sequence from abstract, unchanging principles. Instead, it has been suggested that our lives are composed like music from fortuitous events.

That is the message of Milan Kundera's novel entitled *The Unbearable Lightness of Being.* In it, Tomas, a surgeon, meets and marries his wife, Tereza, through a chain of accidental events that he finds to be both a series of laughable fortuities and a necessitating force. In the course of his life, chance becomes destiny. As he muses on his time with Tereza, he sees six chance happenings that changed his life: "Seven years earlier, a complex neurological case *happened* to have been discovered in Tereza's town. They called in the chief surgeon of Tomas's hospital in Prague for consultation, but the chief surgeon of Tomas's hospital *happened* to be suffering from sciatica, and because he could not move he sent Tomas to the provincial hospital in his place. The town had several hotels, but Tomas *happened* to be given the room in the one where Tereza was employed. He *happened* to have had enough free time before his train left to stop at the hotel restaurant. Tereza *happened* to be on duty, and *happened* to be serving Tomas's table. It had taken six chance happenings to push Tomas towards Tereza, as if he had little inclination to go to her on his own. . . . And that woman, that personification of absolute fortuity, now lay asleep beside him, breathing deeply."[1]

Kundera writes, "Chance and chance alone has a message for us. Everything that occurs out of necessity, everything expected, repeated day in and day out, is mute. Only chance can speak to us. We read its message much as gypsies read the image made by coffee grounds at the bottom of a cup.

"Tomas appeared to Tereza in the hotel restaurant as chance in the absolute. There he sat, poring over an open book, when suddenly he raised his eyes to her, smiled, and said, 'A cognac, please.' . . .

"Necessity knows no magic formulae — they are all left to chance. If a love is to be unforgettable, fortuities must immediately start fluttering down to it like birds to Francis of Assisi's shoulders."[2]

There can be no doubt that we live in a world in which unexpected things happen to us; we are all accident prone for no other reason than that we live in the world. While it is true that things happen to us, it is also true that we can make things happen. We can initiate change as well as undergo it and react to it. Even when something unexpected happens to us, we are the ones who compose the music of our lives from the notes that events make available to us. That composition is the "message" chance has for us; it is the way we incorporate into our lives the fortuities of which Kundera speaks.

1. Kundera, *The Unbearable Lightness of Being,* trans. Michael Henry Heim (New York: Harper & Row, 1991), p. 35.

2. Ibid., pp. 48-49.

The magic in our lives springs from chance, according to Kundera. That is to say, the exciting, transforming events in our lives are not produced by abstract patterns and forms removed from our lives that are said to underlie everything. As persons, we are most ourselves in our spontaneous activities and in the free expressions of our wills. In the fullness of our personal lives, nothing can compel us to be present to each other. Personal presence is the gift of oneself to another who willingly accepts us. We cannot be personally present to each other by intellectual contemplation alone. My contemplation of you cannot be your full presence to me, for my contemplation, being mine and not yours, robs you of the spontaneity which is you. To know *about* your spontaneity is not to know you *in* your spontaneity.

Anything that is meaningful to us must have an experiential relationship with us. Things and events that are meaningful for us must either enter into our experience from the world beyond us or arise in our experience from within us.

Looking at ourselves in rather general terms, we may say that our lives are activities occurring within a field of activities, the latter immediately extending to the world and ultimately to the universe. However, to offer such a description is not to say enough, for, even though we are restricted fields of activity located within wider fields of activity, the activity which is *us* is of a special kind just because it is us. In loose terms, we can say that we are bodies in a world of other bodies, subject to the physical laws of bodies. We move from one place to another through a field of moving bodies when we cross a street with other pedestrians coming toward us and cars going past us; we stub our toe on the bed at night; and we fall from buildings and cliffs. But we somehow are our bodies in a manner different from the way we relate to all other bodies in the world, and we live a life through our bodies that is singularly ours and no one else's in the world. Something special in us enables us to look out on the universe and question it, as well as reflect upon ourselves and ask who we are.

It is a common observation that our lives have a flow to them. The flow is often referred to as a rhythm, and we are aware of rhythmic changes in our lives. Almost all athletes have experienced days when they're "on" and other days when they're "off." The most rigorous training offers no guarantee of the elusive presence. Stepping back from ourselves and trying to analyze what is happening does not help; in fact, it is the sure road to failure. Analysis ties one up by diminishing the spontaneity of the action. We do better by "letting go" than by mental dissection.

When the "pressure is on," the letting go we have described becomes more difficult if not impossible. Athletes also know what it is to "choke," and the athletic experience is not so different from the experience of our everyday lives. Tossing and turning all night in anticipation of tomorrow's decision is similar to serving at match point or having to sink a six-foot putt to win.

There are mornings we get out of bed and proceed through the day with the spontaneity every athlete seeks. We feel on top of things; we are ready to face challenges — we may even look for them; in our activities we feel a certain relaxed exhilaration and enjoyment. We are in a free flow. Most days, however, are different. They are filled with routine activities, and we do them in a routine way. We encounter only minor difficulties, if any, in meeting the expectations of ourselves and others. We think of those as ordinary, typical days. We handle pressures, and we do what we are expected to do. We "stick to it" even if a mild headache or minor intestinal upset bothers us. But there are also times when overwhelming pressures and difficulties confront us. A metastasized cancer threatens us with death; a job is lost; war is declared: disruptions too great to be handled by our accustomed procedures threaten every security we have. We are shaken to our roots. Strangely enough, people often find that, if their problems are overwhelming enough, if they feel the pressures they face are too great for them to handle, they may be led to a new "free flow" through the self-abandonment into which they are forced. Perhaps it would be more accurate to say that, if difficulties are big enough, they may lead to an "ego abandonment" in which the true self is released to be itself.

Before proceeding, we should pause for a moment to acknowledge that there is not just one overruling rhythm and flow to our lives. The dynamism of our lives is a symphony of complementary rhythmic cycles. Molecular rhythms, ultimately traced to our genetic structure, produce what may be called our biological cadence. Sleep patterns, periods of hunger, fertility cycles, attention span, and such complaints as depression all evidence rhythmic patterns. Biological feedback has been used for some time by people trying to maximize their abilities. A person charting his or her biological rhythms certainly does so consciously and with what may be called "ego intentions." At this point I want to say only that our biological rhythms do not exhaust the personal rhythm of our lives. We can speak of rhythmic dimensions in our lives which, although always accompanied by molecular and biological functions, exceed the latter in their nature and significance. In the unique and distinctive aspects of human behavior — in our responsible choices and free self-expression — we may also detect a rhythm of our lives. There is a reason we speak of people marching to the sound of different drummers.

In our most significantly personal activity, it may be said that whenever we are most ourselves — playing our best, meeting our responsibilities, creatively responding to problems confronting us, or creatively expressing ourselves in a new way — we identify the selves we most truly are with the spontaneity by means of which we live. Every fully personal act is spontaneous; the spontaneity to which I refer is the vitality of the act. We feel the act is somehow *us;* we are ourselves through it. Such action is the way we are engaged in the world. It should be no surprise, then, that it is in such action that we as persons are found to be most engaging. We are never more ourselves than when we live with a certain abandon — when, that is, spontaneity replaces calculation. In such action we are free to be ourselves instead of trying to be more than ourselves. In the course of spontaneous activity, we become more than our previous selves because we are drawn beyond ourselves by other people and by our mutual activities in the world.

Spontaneity occurs when we do not have to calculate; although it must be said, parenthetically, that a mathematician can be spontaneous in his calculating. A mathematician who is calculating lives beyond himself in the world of numbers and mathematical functions. He becomes more himself as a mathematician in the spontaneity of his acting; on the other hand, he would be less than himself if his calculations were about how to appear to be a mathematician to others.

In the spontaneous activity we are describing, we can immediately be ourselves because we are not pretending to others — or to ourselves — to be more than we are. Pretense requires that we make an appearance, and to make an appearance requires that we present ourselves to others the way we want them to see us. That, in turn, requires that we quit simply being ourselves, try to look at ourselves as our observers would, and do what they would expect us to do if we were what we want them to think we are! This involves calculation and effort, yes; spontaneous, personal living, no.

Persons reveal themselves in their behavior; we know people by the way they act and express themselves. It is because, in our roots as personal subjects, we are agents that we are more ourselves in the activities through which we express and commit ourselves in the world than we are ourselves in withdrawn reflection alone.

(This is not to say that we should not reflect on our action, as we will see.) In the action in which our personhood is grounded, we are always more than our reflective thought about ourselves.

That truth is the founding insight of what we have come to know as depth psychology. We speak of knowing a person in depth, but what does the phrase mean? It means to know a person in his or her originating, motivating dimensions. It means to know a person interiorly as a subject rather than exteriorly as an object.

Depth psychology tells us that our conscious, reflective lives arise from roots deeper than themselves. Our personal activities are not restricted to conscious awareness; the dynamism of our lives arises from activities of which we are unaware. Unconscious activity occurs beneath our conscious awareness; dreams, for example, tell us something about ourselves. In our personal lives, we, as acting subjects, are more than those aspects of us that can be observed as we observe other objects in the world. For example, my living sight is always more than can be seen either by myself or by others. When I look at myself, the me that looks is more than the me that is seen. The same is true when I think about myself: the self that is thinking is more than the self that is thought. It is *I* who thinks, and the I who is thinking is more than what it thinks. My ability to think is not exhausted by what I have thought in the past or by what I am thinking now.

In our deepest selves, we are unknown and unconscious to ourselves. We become known to ourselves through our activities in the world.

There are many dimensions to human existence, as I have pointed out. In the deepest wellspring of our personal living, we are acting subjects who can never be fully objectified — either to ourselves or to others. As living persons, we are spontaneous sources of activity that transcend everything objective in the world. Because, as persons, we transcend and differ from objects, we can make distinctions among objects from a point of view beyond them. We can compare objects among themselves, and we can look at them from different perspectives, as we do in our sciences. One thing can be known in different ways, and, because of that fact, we can act in different ways toward it. I can admire a painting or slash it to ribbons. It is because we as persons are subjects who transcend objects that we are called by our nature to live decisive lives: we live by deciding what we will do and how we will act. To be a person is to make decisions.

Even though there are physical, objective dimensions of our being, we are not solely related to other objects in the world as no more than one of them. From that fact arises both the grandeur and the tragedy of human life: we can rise above the world in loving concern for others, and we can be crushed in an avalanche. We are located in the world through our bodies, but the "we" who are located, as acting subjects, are more than our bodies. Because we can know objects from different points of view, as I have just mentioned, we can use them and behave toward them in different ways. Our motives, not just their natures, determine what we will do. The fact that we can act from different motives, among which we alone decide, gives a necessarily moral dimension to our lives. Thus it is that the deepest roots of our personal living require that we be moral agents. About that we have no choice.

Our deepest being as personal subjects requires that we be responsible agents making decisions. That is the only way persons can live. No doubt a certain relativity can be found among various concepts of morality — different systems of morality can be found, up to a point, in the history of humankind — but morality of one sort or another defines the human condition. Moral judgments are the acts of living persons deciding what they will do in the various situations in which they find themselves in their lives. Morality is not a veneer added to human life at a certain point in history, when certain cultural conditions have been met, as some would have us believe. Neither is morality a by-product that can be explained by impersonal, physical, or biological causes.

A moral judgment can never be reduced to universal law or a mathematical calculation for the simple reason that, in a moral judgment, nothing can safely be omitted from consideration. Moral judgments are personal judgments. If Kundera is correct, even contingent events can play a necessitating role in a person's life. Tomas, for example, felt a moral obligation to Tereza because of the unnecessary, fortuitous events that bound him to her.

A person's conscience is that person in the totality of his or her being acting responsibly. An "act of conscience" is not the action of a separate faculty we sometimes use and sometimes do not use; it is an action we accomplish by marshaling all the resources we have to make a decision in a given situation. Shall I steal the ring now that no one is looking? Shall I tell the truth about why I missed the meeting or not? Why should I report this income and be taxed on it? Responsible action originates in our wholeness as acting subjects; that is why moral action cannot be completely explained in external terms. Neither can moral action be reduced to something else — merely cultural or psychological phenomena, for example. We live in cultural and psychological contexts that shape our horizons, but those horizons do not replace us as living subjects.

Consciousness always refers to something beyond itself. Consciousness is invariably conscious *of* something. When a person is conscious and awake, he or she is never just conscious. He or she is conscious *of* the book being read, *of* the chair being refinished, *of* the person speaking, *of* the traffic noises outside, *of* the fall of the stock market, *of* a sudden chill in the air, *of* the appointment to which he or she is rushing. A responsible act, as a conscious act, also refers to something beyond itself — to a goal, to a standard, to a person. Consciousness and responsibility go hand in hand, and for that reason a conscious person is a responsible agent.

Both consciousness and responsibility arise from deep, even unconscious dynamic roots. Although human beings have reason and intelligence, they are not totally rational, as life in the world testifies only too well. Given that people have intelligence, we expect them to act intelligently, but it does not take many years of life for any intelligent person to expect that expectation to be frustrated.

Although our expectations of other people frequently lead to disappointment, if not despair, the nature of our conscious, personal lives allows us no alternative to attempting to live for who we are with other people for who they are. There is no ultimate alternative to human beings relating to each other and having to live together. How that is to be done is the problem.

3

The Minimalist View of Reality

WE HAVE spoken of accidental events in our lives. There may be people who have not been "in an accident," but there is no one who has not accidentally done something unintended at one time or another, or has not had something accidentally happen to him or her.

An accident is an accident because it is singular and un-planned; it is an event that happens suddenly and without warn-ing. We slip; we are hit; the door blows shut before we get back inside; we meet a friend in a city neither of us has visited before. Lack of preparation and expectation is the rule for accidents.

Other than their unexpectedness, accidents have no rules. Their arbitrariness is the most characteristic and destructive thing about them. They have no respect for persons or propriety. The most respected person in the community, the high school principal who was everybody's friend, was accidentally caught in the crossfire of a teenage gang war as he helped a youngster cross the street after school. Not only was there no reason for his death, but there was every reason why it should not have occurred. The speeding bullet would hit whatever was in its path, and the principal happened to have been the one who was there. The gang members were firing at each other, not at him.

Because of the arbitrary way accidents enter our lives, they are disruptions. They change things. An accident cannot be a part of anyone's plan; a "planned accident" is a contradiction in terms. Something may be planned to look like an accident, but it is another case where looks are deceiving. If I lose my money on the way to the bank, my plan to deposit it is defeated. I had planned to keep my money in the safest place possible; I had not planned to lose it. The accidental loss of the money changes the order of my life. A radical element of disorder has broken into the ordered chain of events I had intended. The meaning of my life has been upset by something I had not counted on. If the money is not found and returned, the loss will be a new element I will have to incorporate into the meaning of my life that I can foresee for the future.

People we happened to meet, books we happened to read, a defeat that surprised us, a lucky break we had not counted on — these are the events that are most pivotal for us. Structures that are always present and events that follow each other with uninterrupted regularity may be considered the floor we walk upon in the world, but we would rather find another person to talk to or dance with on the floor than sit all evening staring at the floor.

There is a singularity to our lives that makes every person different from and unsubstitutable for anyone else. Each one of us is special to himself or herself, and the people we like best are the ones who treat us for the special persons we are. We like people who look us in the eye when they are talking to us and who know our name. People speak to *us* when they speak to us in our singularity rather than addressing us as if we were no more than an individual representative of a group. Generic distinctions, whether they be by race, language, occupation, sex, or social class, miss us for who we are in our intimate selves. As persons, we want meaning that is immediately ours; we want the meaning of our lives to be as singularly ours as are our lives themselves.

The accidental, in its singularity, speaks to us in our singularity. What is accidental says something special to us as the special persons we are at a special time; what is regular and structured says the same thing all the time to everybody, thus making time and our uniqueness — the essence of our lives — meaningless. A truly personal message is always a communication of one person's singularity to another's. Nothing has more meaning for *him* than a love note from *her, now,* just when *he* wants it.

If we act prudently and exercise foresight, we may be able to prevent accidents, but as long as we live in the world there is nothing that can totally insure us against accidents. "Accident insurance" does not prevent accidents from happening; it simply offers additional resources after an accident has occurred to help the individuals affected resume the lives that were altered by the accident. Insurance that comes only after an accident has occurred is hardly accident insurance in the most welcome sense!

Accidents are arbitrary interruptions of the sequence of our lives. Persons, on the other hand, are conscious, reflective agents who set goals for themselves and try to achieve them. The goal may be to understand the ultimate nature of physical reality in high-energy physics, or it may be no more than going out to dinner this evening. Either goal, or any other goal that we can propose, presupposes that the world around us is at least partially structured and stable. There can be no such thing as a goal or an intention in chaotic disorder. We ourselves are ordered wholes, and there is a consistent wholeness — we call it character — in the lives of the people we most admire.

We live by meaning, for there is meaning to our lives. In our scientific pursuits, we try to discover meaning in reality, and, where reality seems to dumbfound us by fortuitous and un-expected events, we attempt to give meaning to that which confronts us. That is how we handle accidents. When Tennyson has Ulysses say, "I am a part of all that I have met," he means that Ulysses has at least partially contributed a meaning of his own to the events of his life; he was not completely controlled by what happened to him. When Ulysses exhorts his companions, "Come, my friends, 'tis not too late to seek a newer world," the world he refers to is the one he will make, not just receive at the hands of fate.

The message that chance events have for us is revealed in the way we incorporate them into our lives; their message is heard through the thematic use we make of them in the composing of our lives. We are able to give accidents meaning, even though, in themselves, they stand outside our intentions. "Why me?" is our first thought when something goes wrong; subsequently our thoughts turn to making the best out of what is left to us.

While we must incorporate whatever happens to us into our lives, even if such incorporation requires our giving meaning to an event that disrupts our original intentions, we must also recognize that even the most arbitrary and disruptive accident says something to us by itself. Every accident opens a new aspect of reality to us; accidents are the way in which external reality breaks into our lives and forces us to recognize its existence. The immediate message every accident brings to us is that, because of it, we must live differently. Accidents lay an undeniable demand upon us. If a football player loses a leg or an opera singer accidentally damages her throat, their lives change. Accidents, of themselves, demand that we live and behave differently; how we change our lives is where we enter the picture as givers of meaning.

In circumstances over which we have no control, the way in which we incorporate them into our lives furnishes meaning for them; there are times that we must simply will an overriding meaning into events. In the more normal course of human life, however, we search for the consistent interrelations and the coherence that the external world embodies in itself. Predictability is the goal of scientific research. To be able to predict the events that will follow from our actions shows both our understanding of nature and our control of it.

Viewed in their totality, our lives are always a combination of chance events and predictable regularities, and, as long as we and the world remain what we are, it appears that we will never be able completely to remove accident and chance from our lives.

The bipolar structure of the necessary and the contingent is well illustrated in the area of human health, and it is to the latter subject that we may now turn our attention. To inquire about the nature of human health is to inquire about the nature of being human. Health is not something that exists in itself; it is persons or animals or plants that are healthy. Health is a condition found in a living subject, and the nature of the subject determines the nature of its health. How health is to be achieved varies from subject to subject: while veterinary medicine has much in common with human medicine, for example, a sick person is not normally rushed to the nearest veterinarian. In no case is an ill person rushed to the nearest botanist.

In a pluralistic republic such as the United States, responsibility for the medical care of its citizens exposes tensions and difficulties in the basic concept of government itself. An examination of those tensions reveals not just problems of government, however; it also offers insights into the nature of our lives as persons — the source of all governmental problems!

Decisions about health care challenge the very concept of the liberal state, according to Fred M. Frohock. He writes, "The dream of liberalism is governing with neutral procedures, of finding and using those rules and principles that are outside the domain of values specifying the good life in human communities. In conflicts between holistic and allopathic medical values, the state meets the terms of the liberal ideal with regulations that do not depend on the particular worldviews of either community but rather on a set of procedures that are reasonably empty of substance."[1]

Professor Frohock traces the last several centuries of medical care, from the bloodletting of the eighteenth and early nineteenth centuries, through the development of homeopathy, which originated in the second half of the nineteenth century, on through the allopathic medicine practiced in the twentieth century. Homeopathic medicine was generally based upon the principle that disease could be cured by ingesting infinitesimal amounts of drugs that produced the symptoms of the illness. Homeopathic medicine spawned inoculations against disease. Flu shots are one of its benefits.

Modern medicine, according to Frohock, is marked by identifying and treating illness in the context of physiology, seeing the relations between disease and bodily states as a causal one, and relying upon the generic applicability of the laws of physiology to all human bodies. Allopathic medicine, therapy that fights disease through agents that produce effects different from the effects produced by the disease, had its ascendancy in the twentieth century. Chemotherapy for cancer patients is a good example of it. Near the close of the twentieth century, molecular biology and genetic engineering offer therapeutic possibilities far exceeding anything known in the past.

Homeopathic, allopathic, and genetic medicine are not, however, the only therapies in the field. As health has come to be understood more and more in terms of the whole person, holistic medicine and therapies have become more widely advocated. What is generally referred to as holistic medicine denotes a wide

1. Frohock, *Healing Powers: Alternative Medicine, Spiritual Communities, and the State* (Chicago: University of Chicago Press, 1992), pp. 31-32. Subsequent references will be made parenthetically in the text.

range of theories and therapies, and primary among them, for our purposes, are the practices known as faith healing or spiritual healing. As Frohock puts it, faith healing arouses hostility in those committed to the scientific method by setting "a mood that is primarily subjective, not rigorously structured to suit the objective aims of science" (p. 135). Holistic therapies regard individuals in holistic terms, which means that a patient's body is not treated as no more than an individual instance of a general or generic type; instead, each patient is regarded as the unique, singular subject he or she is. There is no such thing as a "regular" broken leg, for example; an X ray of a broken bone does not reveal the significance of the fracture in the life of the person who has it.

In some ways the therapy employed by Alcoholics Anonymous is one of the least specific therapies of those which may be said to involve spiritual healing. AA does not require that one believe in a certain kind of God; no specific creedal adherence or spiritual outlook is demanded in its program. But belief that there is some higher power than oneself is an absolute prerequisite. Frohock's discussion of AA offers several suggestions that will be helpful for our future considerations. He writes that "the controlling thought is that something outside of the self, some external being, is needed for the salvation that AA offers. . . . Therapy is successful as the individual retreats from explicit or linear forms of thought and begins to rely on the unconscious, on the deep intuitive sense that AA sees as capable of apprehending some external reality. It is not inaccurate to say that the discrete and rational individual assumed in so much of contemporary thought is abandoned, and even on occasion seen as the source of the pathology that AA methods attempt to heal" (p. 104). It is noteworthy that Frohock uses the term "salvation" to describe AA's goal, and his reference to the higher power appealed to as an "external being" is a topic about which I will have more to say later.

According to Frohock, the most important belief for those who believe in religion and spiritual healing is that human life is found within a reality larger than itself which is ruled by purpose or design rather than by chance. In such a view, first principles are held to be discovered or revealed rather than chosen. They arise from a source beyond us. Also, "instead of the linear forms of reasoning expressed most strongly in deductive models, belief in a larger reality requires a narrative frame of communication in which truth is deciphered rather than presented. . . . Interpretive or narrative reasoning . . . is forced upon spiritual thought by the ineffable nature of spiritual knowledge. Once one accepts the truth of a reality outside human experience, narrative modes of expression are inevitable. But the narrative itself cannot establish truth. One first must believe in order for such reasoning to work" (pp. 205-6).

The interpretive and narrative reasoning forced on communication about spiritual realities is the source of conflict between scientific and spiritual communities. Here we meet again the bipolar structure of the necessary and the contingent in human experience to which I previously referred. Science deals with the necessary and the repeatable; narrative describes the singular and the contingent. In science, explanations proceed deductively as conclusions are shown to follow necessarily from premises; the same conclusions always follow from given premises. In medicine, when a singular and unexpected recovery occurs, it is called a "spontaneous healing." But "spontaneity" is not a cause of healing, for it explains nothing. It *describes* something; the spontaneous is conveyed by inductive narrative rather than understood by deductive reductions.

To the extent that medicine tries to remain scientific in the face of spontaneous healing, the healing is said to be due to unknown causes. Once premises are set up — the principles of physiology, for example, in medicine — nothing foreign to the premises can be admitted into their domain. The phenomena that scientific medicine deals with must be extendable to all human bodies. When something happens that is not extendable — when consequences occur that cannot be predicted or deduced — the scientific mind will say that some causal factor is operating that has yet to be discovered. Thus the search for causes goes on as unexpected events occur.

Scientific method is based on predictability. The singular has no meaning for it. The experiment of one researcher must be verifiable by any other researcher who sets up the same conditions and follows the same procedures. There is a history of science; it is a fascinating story that recounts hunches that were followed, mistakes that were made, and leads that did not turn out. Narrative tells us about scientists' imaginations and guesses, their hopes and fears, because it describes what has happened, but only repeatable experiments tell us the truth of science.

Scientific experiments are attempts to disprove hypotheses, and the attempt to disprove hypotheses has been offered as a definition of scientific method. Only hypotheses capable of being disproved have any meaning in the physical sciences, for, if a hypothesis does not say something specific enough to be disproved, it does not say anything specific enough to make a positive difference if it *is* true. If there is no experimental way to indicate that a theory may be wrong, there is no significance in saying that it is correct. Years may go by before an experiment can be set up or before the conditions necessary to test a hypothesis can be found — as was the case with Einstein's general theory of relativity — but sooner or later some crucial experiment must be found for a hypothesis if it is to be a meaningful scientific building block. The lack of falsifiability of religious claims makes them nonscientific. If a person believes in spiritual healing, he or she can continue to believe in it whether a person prayed for is healed or not.

Frohock concludes that spiritual therapy and conventional therapy involve two incompatible realities. It is that incompatibility which poses a problem for liberal government. In society at large, the conflict between opposing views of reality results in pluralism, but, if society is to be integrated, some view — and so some persons — must dominate other views and other persons. The difficulty is that there is no common language between the disputing communities which allows a compromise to be reached. In spite of that fact, there come times when it is felt that the state must step into a disputed situation in order to protect its citizens. What is the duty of the state when Christian Scientist parents will not allow their child with a burst appendix to be operated upon? No matter what its theoretical intentions about remaining neutral, if the state forces the parents to send the child to the hospital for the operation, the state has not been neutral in its actions.

Disputes about the treatment of illness spring from differing views about the nature of reality among various communities within the state. The liberal state tries to stand above such disputes by providing a civil forum within which differing points of view can coexist and confront each other, but, by its actions if not its intentions, the state cannot remain totally neutral. Thus, says Frohock, it is that "a state confined to regulating the domain of bodies, and historically committed to minimal regulation and individual freedoms, must also rest on a minimalist concept of reality" (p. 267).

To say that the liberal state has a minimalist concept of reality in its domain of regulating bodily behavior is to say that the state has a minimalist view not only of the human body but also of the human person. Human persons *are* their bodies; they do not just have bodies. There are no persons who are unlocated in reality, and it is our bodies which locate us in the world. If we want to find someone, we go to the place we know his or her body to be.

The state, in its attempt to retain neutrality, regards its citizens as entities having bodies, rather than regarding them in their intimate personal lives located by their bodies. It is because the state abstracts itself from the fully personal dimensions of the bodily lives of its citizens that sex education in the public schools causes so much furor. Many believe that, with no more than the minimalistic intention to protect the physical health of its citizens, the state should, in its schools, instruct the youth of the country about how to avoid sexually transmitted diseases. From the minimalist point of view, that is not difficult to do: one simply describes sexual differences, sexual acts, and prophylactic procedures. The unfortunate thing is that here again, in spite of the intent of remaining neutral, such actions by the state appear to many to constitute the advocacy of a lower rather than a higher view of human sex. The meaning of sex appears to be reduced to no more than its act.

It may be argued that, in taking the minimalist view of the human body, the state is not trying to reduce persons in themselves to the minimal level of the state's choice. Rather, it may be maintained that it is precisely because human persons have dimensions of a higher order than their bodies that the state tries to absent itself from those areas as a mark of its recognition of the sovereignty of its individual citizens and their families. Being located in the world by our bodies, we cannot help having different perspectives in the world on the world, but, although the perspectival nature of our life arises from our bodily location, the perspectives we incarnate need not be reduced to bodily functions. "To be located by" our bodies does not necessarily mean "to be reduced to" our bodies. There are those who hold that a human being can be reduced to physiological functions and by-products of those functions, but the liberal state does not necessarily endorse that minimalist view in its governing functions.

The minimalist concept of reality upon which the liberal state governs can actually be looked at as accidental to the state. The concept is something into which the state is forced for reasons external to the state's intentions. The situation is not unlike pushing a person to the edge of a rooftop; if one is pushed too far, his or her body will obey the gravitational law of falling bodies, whether the person involved intends to or not. The displeasure of a majority about a certain issue in a liberal state may push the state into an action from which inevitable results follow regardless of what the state would theoretically wish to have happen.

According to Frohock, in the pluralistic society found in a liberal state, the goal of neutrality or minimal value commitment on behalf of the state is founded upon the state's presumption — until proven wrong — that its citizens are isolated and competent individuals. Citizens are presumed to be both independent and self-sufficient. It is the recognition of the isolated competence of individuals that grounds the hands-off policy of government. Respect for individual competence founds the right of citizens to be left alone in whatever they do in their lives, as long as what they do does not interfere with the ability of other people to exercise the same privilege in their lives.

States differ from persons because they are collective entities composed of many persons, while a person is a singular, non-collective whole. Plato, in his *Republic,* asserted that the personal virtues of wisdom, courage, justice, and temperance were "writ large" in the life of the state, and so could be seen and studied more easily on the larger scale than on the smaller. In so thinking, however, he misrepresented both the lives of persons and the lives of states. He neglected the differences between singular and collective existence. Singular persons live and make decisions differently than collective, political states.

Plato's error does not prevent other people from making the same mistake he made, although they may make it with less consideration than he gave the subject. In our own day, enthusiastic support for nonjudgmental pluralism at the state level seems so appropriate to the human condition that there are some — whether they have considered all the consequences or not — who try to adopt the same attitude as a personal ethic. Nonjudgmental respect for others and the nonjudgmental pluralism of society resulting from it are the high ideals of such an attempt.

As praiseworthy as the ideals may be, however, it is questionable whether they are compatible with the life of a human person when that life is considered in its depth and singularity. Successful personal living is not an attempt to escape identity. Quite the contrary. It is by means of their lives that persons try to establish their identities, actually creating themselves by the decisions and choices they make. From the point of view of government, the liberal state may be its best self when it is most anonymous in the life of its citizens, but persons seek anonymity when they want to be less than themselves rather than their full selves. I have observed that every person is special to herself or himself, and we feel we are best known by others when they treat us for the special persons we are. But no burglar wants to be known for the special person he is; he seeks anonymity in the darkness of night just so he will not be known.

To a large extent, persons can choose their identities; an identity cannot be chosen ready-made, but, as I have mentioned, we make our personal identities through the responsible actions we choose in the course of our lives. The core of our personhood is revealed in our responsible choices. We are most who we are in the exercise of our free will; would it not be a loss, then, to have a person freely choose, as a model of his or her personal life, what the liberal state is forced to do because of purely external circumstances? The neutrality of the liberal state is achieved by the state's holding itself at one remove from the lives of its citizens. If its citizens try to make the model of the state the model for their personal lives, they will be trying to live lives at one remove from themselves by themselves. They will try to be to themselves only what they are to the state; they will know themselves only as they are known by the state; they will, in other words, substitute external relations for internal intentions as the basis for their lives.

The difficulty we have just described is based upon a category mistake: one kind of being is confused with another. In the instance before us, a collective society is confused with a singular person. The collective nature of a state, even though it is composed of persons, makes it less than personal in many ways. The processes by which a state maintains itself are different from the activities of a person, although there may appear to be impressive similarities between the two. We talk about the behavior of states, and we speak of the behavior of persons, but the intrinsic nature of the behavior is very different in the two instances. States govern by process, while persons live by actions; "agency" in government connotes bureaucratic offices and personal anonymity, while "agency" in personal life connotes singular responsibility and identity. When I act as a person, because I am myself in the action, I am — and I want to be — responsible for what I do; when an agency acts, on the other hand, personal responsibility is impossible to determine. Bureaucracy is to personal responsibility what darkness is to a burglar.

Knowledge grows as human beings are able to make distinctions, and it is with considerable justification that "to know" has been equated with "to distinguish." When our distinctions are not clear, our knowledge is confused. Human beings have never had as many distinctions available to them in their history as they have today; the result is that, in sum, human beings have never known as much as they know today. But the summary accumulation of knowledge does not prevent individual mistakes from being made, and one of the hottest centers of conflicting claims is that concerning the nature of the human person.

That conflict brings us back to the question with which we began: "Who are we?" I shall now try to answer that question with an analysis of my own.

4

Accepting Ourselves and Discovering God

As we proceed in our attempt to discover who we are, we must, if we are to succeed, let our most immediate awareness of ourselves speak to us. That will not be easy, for we are used to considering external reality — and ourselves — from theoretical points of view that furnish us with concepts and structures we bring to our consideration. What we need to do now is to let our awareness of ourselves speak to us for what it is in itself before we apply any theory or objective analysis to it. We need to look at ourselves as we feel at home with ourselves, which is to say we need to look at those dimensions of our experience which are so immediate and basic that there is no alternative to them as long as we recognize ourselves to be ourselves. We must let ourselves — as we are *given* to ourselves and as we *find* ourselves — speak to us before we try to analyze ourselves. That is a legitimate priority because our ability to make analyses of things, including ourselves, arises from the selves we are in the first place. We do not analyze ourselves into existence.

There is no doubt that we feel most ourselves in our spontaneous activity; our lives are at their best in their integral spontaneity, when we are whole and acting. In our lives as persons, it is important that the integrity and spontaneity I have just mentioned qualify each other. Persons are complex wholes with many different aspects and dimensions; we can literally be "broken down," and when that happens we are not ourselves. Because breakdowns occur, the action of someone, just because it is spontaneous, is not automatically personal. A sensual shock — be it from a car crash, an electrical contact, or a chemical injection — can so affect an individual that, although he or she reacts spontaneously, the action is not truly personal. The action to which I refer is the action of someone who is "gathered" and fully functioning in all dimensions of his or her existence.

Considering ourselves again, then, when we feel most ourselves, where are our true selves located?

I have already given the answer. The most basic sense of identity we know is located in our immediate awareness of ourselves as the subjects of our experience. We have seen that the "I" each one of us is as a living subject is always located beyond the "me" that we or others can observe as an object.

Although depth is a physical category, there is no substitute for using it in describing our most original selves as subjects. I as an acting subject lie "beneath" myself as an observable person or ego behaving in certain ways. Deep within me there is a source of activity, an agent whose spontaneous aspiration I know myself to be; that is where I recognize my personal identity to be founded. Such knowledge of myself is immediate, but there is also an indirect aspect to it. As a subject, I know myself indirectly when I know objects, for I am aware that whatever knowledge I have is *mine* — but, as I have repeatedly said, I can never completely become an object to myself.

The subject that is the source of my personal identity lies beneath, and expresses itself through, my conscious activities. As a person, I also have an ego; it is my conscious self-identity. Yet, as we have seen, the subject that knows itself and that knows about itself is always more than the self it knows; the self that looks is always more than the self that is seen. We are deep sources of action that express themselves through, but can never be reduced to, the different dimensions of our behavior we describe and distinguish in our self-analyses.

What is at the core of our selfhood? We are agents whose activity, arising from the unconscious, wells up over the threshold of consciousness into our conscious, responsible lives with each other in the world. The deepest source of our lives is not an unknown that will someday be known; its unavailability to us partially defines us. Feeling at home with ourselves as that source of activity and being aware of its role — truly living from it and with it as the root of our conscious lives — is a key to being the full persons we are and are meant to be.

Our conscious, responsible activity comes from, and is a manifestation of, a source of activity lying beyond that portion of our lives for which we are responsible. To reveal responsibly our pre-responsible spontaneity is the challenge to which we are called as persons; we most completely respond to that challenge in the conscious acts of our will.

Willing arises spontaneously within us and reveals something basic about us. When we first recognize ourselves as persons, willing is an aspect of ourselves we find already present. Willing is a manifestation of who we are; it is not an arbitrary activity for whose presence we are responsible. That is to say, our willing is not a derivative, sometime activity in which we may or may not indulge; it is a manifestation of our deepest selves, and for that reason we necessarily will ourselves and what appears good to us. Sometimes the human will is said to be a separate faculty along with such other faculties as reason, the physical senses, and the emotions. It is more adequate to say that when we refer to a person's will — his or her free will — we are simply referring to the spontaneity of the person as a subject being itself; we are referring to the conscious agency of a subject as that activity is contrasted with the physical processes of reality found both within our bodies and beyond our bodies in the world.

In our full lives as consciously acting subjects, we are able to exercise responsibility within our willing, but we are not responsible for our willing itself. Willing is given to us as one with the gift of ourselves to ourselves. Willing is present in us as a constitutive element of our lives, and, because its presence is one with our presence, it has a basic givenness and identity that must simply be recognized and respected for what they are.

Our willing cannot be reduced to something more basic than itself or be derived from something different from itself and still be itself. Before we could explain it in terms of something different from itself, for example, we would already be expressing ourselves as subjects through it in a manner preventing it from being no more than an object of our investigation. After all, the act of will by which we begin an investigation and keep it going is never the act of will we investigate when we reflect upon our will. Willing is a manifestation of our deepest selves as subjects; as such, it lies at the root of our personal consciousness, which is why we identify the deepest desires of our wills with ourselves.

There is no doubt that we reveal who we are in our willing, but more must be said. When we become attentive to our willing in the primacy and immediacy in which we recognize ourselves in it, we discover our willing to be an activity that is open both in its origin and in its goal. What is the origin of our will? Because we never discover ourselves without discovering we are already willing, we cannot account, by ourselves, for the presence of willing in us. We never begin to will for the first time for no other reason than that it is our will to begin willing. As persons, we have no choice about willing; because our willing does not come from us, we apprehend, in the immediacy of its presence, that its ultimate origin lies beyond us.

When we turn our attention to the object of our willing instead of its origin, we discover that we are led beyond ourselves once more. The object of our will, like the origin of our will, always lies beyond us. We desire what we do not have, but, no matter what we desire, we also know that no object we will ever completely satisfies us. The common testimony of the stirrings of the human will throughout the collective and individual histories of humankind is that we are never satisfied. We always want more. Any object that we will, by virtue of being an object, is fixed and limited. For that reason it fails to satisfy the unlimited spontaneity of our being. That is why, for example, sexual appetite is never satisfied with another person, no matter how attractive the other person may be, if that person is regarded only as an object of appetite. There is ample evidence that being married to a beautiful woman does not satisfy the appetite of some men; they still desire as many other conquests as they can make.

If, in our most immediate awareness of ourselves as acting subjects, we discover our lives to be open to something beyond us in both our origin and our goal, a major truth about us is exposed. We are not — and we cannot be — ourselves by ourselves. Stated this generally, the truth may seem no more than a truism: everyone knows — even the most self-centered person — that living in the world makes us dependent upon the world. After all, the world is the setting for our lives, and only in the world and by its resources can we stay alive. The full significance of the truth before us comes in the more precise specification of exactly *what* it is we depend upon and *how* we depend upon it. We are ourselves only in the world, but is it only the world and the things of the world that we depend upon?

If we follow the lines of this analysis, we must say that the world and the goods of the world we can acquire will never be able adequately to satisfy our needs as living subjects. We need more than the world, because, even though we are in the physical world, we are more than that world. It sounds rather biblical, but it may nevertheless be true. Not coming from ourselves and tending beyond ourselves in the basic striving we discover ourselves to be, we, in our very being, speak a dependence on an action beyond us that does not share our limitations. *In willing ourselves,* we realize that we are dependent on something beyond ourselves within our willing, and nothing less than that sufficient source can furnish an adequate goal for our limitless longing.

The unconscious depths of our spontaneous being immediately relate us to a source beyond us. Knowing ourselves in our internal reference beyond ourselves, we implicitly know ourselves in our ultimate origin — God — and, knowing ourselves in that origin, we also know our goal, the only thing that can fully satisfy our needs in the end — God. We cannot help freely moving, as toward our goal, toward the origin from which we arise. We are a dependent freedom: we are free to make ourselves, but only within certain limits that have been given to us.

Because we are a limited, dependent freedom, we can be and become our true selves only by freely using (cooperating with and depending upon) the source of the freedom from which we come. We are dependent agents, and we are most ourselves in acknowledging, rather than denying, that dependency.

There are those who say that to acknowledge the existence of God beyond us limits our freedom, compromising it and preventing it from being itself. But that is not the case. The existence of God does not limit our freedom because God does not stand outside our freedom as an object. It is in our immediate awareness of the spontaneity we are that we become aware of God's presence within us enabling us to be ourselves. In that intentional awareness, we do not jump from an activity sufficient in itself to something beyond it that restricts and limits its being its full self. It is in the immediate fullness of the activity we are that we become aware of the intentional presence of a source beyond us and in us enabling us to be what we are, for we do not come from ourselves. We will *for* ourselves but not *from* ourselves.

God and I as persons do not relate to each other as objects. My knowledge of God and my life with God are realized (made "objective") not by my relating to him as I would to an external object through the use of objectifying ideas, but by my living as subject in the living presence of God as subject. When we relate this way, neither God nor I is or can become an object for the other.

God is the source who, in the gift of the spontaneous aspiration by means of which I always will myself (will, that is, what I take as good for me and what I want), enables me to be a person. Any knowledge of God as an external object outside me is bound to be not merely inadequate but positively false and misleading.

We may now be in a position better to appreciate the significance of Fred Frohock's remark that the therapy of Alcoholics Anonymous, for example, is built upon a deep and intuitive awareness of an external reality beyond the struggling self. *Intuitive* is a much-maligned word in our day; when we speak of someone's intuition, we normally refer to a hunch the person has about something that may or may not be true. People take chances on their intuitive hunches, and gamblers are especially known for playing their intuitions. To say that a therapy, or anything else, is based on an intuition seems to us to indicate that it is based on something blindly assumed because no rational evidence can be found for it.

I have avoided using *intuition* or any of its variables in this discussion precisely because of the prejudice against it and the common misunderstanding of it. I could have said that we intuit the immediate apprehension of ourselves that I have been describing, but, if I had, I would not by that fact have been saying that we are following only one hunch among others about something which may or may not be factual. In this analysis I would use *intuitive* in the same way that Frohock uses it to describe AA therapy — as the opposite of *deducible*. The most immediate awareness we can have of ourselves may be called intuitive because it reveals existence so immediately ours that there is nothing prior to it — or better known than it is — from which it could be derived. It cannot be explained by anything prior to it.

The apprehension of ourselves about which I have been speaking is an awareness of ourselves so immediately present that there is no alternative to it. The apprehension is something about which we cannot make impartial judgments or construct abstract arguments; we cannot relate impartially to it or abstract ourselves from it because it reveals what we *are*. We may consciously recognize or not recognize the features of our existence that I have been describing — we may realize who we are or not realize who we are in our depths — but because those depths constitute our being, whether we know it or not, our lives themselves are our commitment to them. If we try to live in a manner that contradicts or ignores our basic constitution, consequences will follow in the internal tensions and stresses that such living produces. Thus it is that the type of isolated, rationalistic individualism so frequently assumed in our culture is seen by Alcoholics Anonymous to lie at the source of the addictive escape addressed in its therapy.

Before continuing, it will be helpful to observe and comment upon Frohock's remark that the ultimate reality involved in AA therapy is something external to human beings and something whose presence is rooted in the human unconscious. I have called attention to the purposeful ambiguity that AA advocates in order to be as inclusive as possible in its clientele. Such ambiguity is not necessary for us, however, and some of the possibilities it allows would prejudice and contradict the consistent position we are trying to establish.

As I have indicated, while it is necessary to recognize a God who transcends us and is beyond us in his transcendence, it is vital to realize that God is not beyond us or outside us as an object. That is why we cannot know God through objectifying ideas. God is a subject who in the free gift of his will enables us to be the freely willing subjects we are. It is in God's difference from us, in his all-sufficiency, that he transcends us, but in the act of his creative will God is also immanently present in us, as a subject to a subject, enabling us to be who we are.

We are so used to thinking of relations in objective terms that we miss the uniqueness of our relation with God — and with each other as persons. The subject-never-to-be-object that each of us is in our deepest selves can be itself only with other subjects, never with objects. The self as subject is not destroyed but is missed when considered as if it were an object; it can reveal something of itself through objects, but it can never completely be itself with objects.

Unlike objects, which relate externally to each other and exclude each other by being themselves, subjects are more themselves with others through intimate, internal (willed) relations. They help constitute each other internally, rather than standing outside each other by exclusion or submission.

The spontaneous center of our lives is the dimension of our being involved in our relation with God. We are related to God in our deepest roots; the relationship is more basic than words because it arises from a source within us deeper than words. God is in our lives from beneath and within us as we are subjects, not as an object beyond us. God is the source of our action, not its object. We become aware of God's presence in our lives when we become aware of the dependent mode in which we are ourselves. Our willing does not conflict with the presence of God's all-sufficient will within us; rather, our willing depends upon it. In our immediate awareness of the dependent activity we are, we discover God present enabling us to be ourselves.

Our awareness of ourselves in the activity of our will is the key to our recognition of God's presence in our lives. We discover our dependence on God in the willing of ourselves, but, once we discover that dependence, we understand that it cannot be limited to our willing. It permeates every aspect of our being. Willing may be the key to our first discovering God in our lives, but, once discovered, that key unlocks the significance of our whole being.

There are great advantages to discovering God's free will within the action of our free wills, because by making that discovery we rule out the temptation of trying to reduce our relationship with God to one of abstract knowledge alone. Because our relationship with God is anchored in the deepest spontaneity of our being, there is more to belief than its intellectual object. That is why religious living cannot be derived from an analysis of its object. Life with God is different from thinking about God.

I remarked earlier that the way we make our relationship with God "objective" is by living with God as a subject lives with a subject rather than by trying to relate to God as an object beyond us. The reality underlying that statement also offers the reason why our awareness of God cannot be reduced to our ideas of God. Ideas objectify reality: we hold ideas in our minds, or, as metaphor puts it, ideas are held before our mind's eye. But anything we are able to hold before us becomes, by that very act, an object for us. Thus the act obscures rather than reveals the God who cannot be an object.

When referring to the living God, we come closer to the truth when we say "God is present" than when we say "God exists." The presence of someone makes a difference to us. The existence of a person in himself or herself, in contrast to that person's presence in our lives, is something we can admit without its making any difference to us at all. A god who can be admitted to exist but whose existence makes no difference to those acknowledging it is not God. God is God only because he makes a difference. To offer proof that God does not exist is not a victory for atheism; it is a victory for the recognition of the only God who is God, the God who does not just exist in himself but who is *present* everywhere and who makes a difference everywhere by his presence.

Personal presence overflows objective expression and bare existence and cannot be reduced to either of them. Because God is a living subject who can be known only as a subject, God relates to us and reveals himself to us only as we are living subjects. To the extent that we deny our nature as subjects by treating ourselves and those around us as objects, we diminish our ability to recognize God in our lives. The perfection of God known in theology as the divine "simplicity" is the human acknowledgment that there is nothing in God that can be separated from him and be objectified for our inspection. God is a mystery whose transcendent wholeness and perfection prevent our ever having clear ideas of him compatible with the limiting structures of our thought.

Our ideas obviously cannot grasp the God who is beyond our grasp. That fact does not, however, prevent God from speaking actually — that is, historically — to us. Christians believe that God reveals himself to human beings in the concrete fullness and singularity of historical events. The God whose being is the spontaneous action of love reveals himself in the action of speaking, which is why Christians recognize God's revealing Word to be the action of a life rather than a proposition — or a group of propositions — about God. God's Word spoken to human beings is the Word made flesh in the life of Jesus of Nazareth; God's Word is a living Word that cannot be reduced to static concepts or formal pronouncements. The living God can be known only in the living action of his presence; anything less is not he.

In summary we may say that in distinctly Christian faith, God's self-disclosure is the basis of everything known about God.

Such self-disclosure is revelatory, but it is never a revelation. If God's self-disclosure were a revelation, the action of his presence would be reduced to a thing or an object, something with its own existence that we could examine and draw conclusions from in its own right. If that were possible, revelation would be something we could receive and examine as we receive and examine the world of objects within which we live. However, God's revelatory self-disclosure can never be separated from his living presence. God speaks only in the actuality of his presence; consequently, his speaking can never be reduced to something he has said and to which appeal can be made as an object inherited from the past. Self-disclosure is always a living activity if the disclosing person is present with us, and with God there is no other alternative. God's self-disclosure is a speaking, never a thing spoken.

The static can have no part in the God whose free, spontaneous love is the source of the spontaneity centering our lives. Awareness of God is always awareness of God present to us calling us beyond ourselves into the spontaneity of his all-sufficient love. Anything less than the movement of our lives beyond themselves into the unfathomable love who is God is less than a relation with the living God.

Nothing less than that relationship will be our concern as we proceed.

5

Are There Any Rules?

HERE we are — we have arrived again at our starting point.

We have talked a bit about the world in which we live, and we have found it to be a world containing elements of necessity and chance, sickness and health, fulfillment and disappointment, fortune and misfortune. We have gone on to discover that, although we as persons live in the world, we are also different from it. While it is true that our bodies locate us in the interconnected web of physical energy we call the universe, we are not completely submerged in the physical systems constituting the universe. As subjects, we are a different kind of being from the objects of the world: as subjects we are able to look at the world, at life, and even at ourselves from different perspectives. Purposes arising within us — and which are ours alone — enable us to see a given object from different points of view and thus use the object in different ways for our different purposes. We may eat an apple, throw it, paint it, or analyze its chemical, nutritional, or atomic structure, just to mention a few possibilities. To be a human being is to make decisions.

Perhaps the most difficult topic we discussed was our immediate awareness of ourselves, for almost all of our cultural dispositions and scientific activities lead us away from such self-recognition. Objectivity is our proclaimed goal. We desire objects; we seek objects; we acquire objects; we control objects; and, in the best knowledge we can have of ourselves, we are told that we must be objective if we are truly to know ourselves.

Awareness of ourselves as subjects rather than objects causes us problems, because, although such awareness is immediate, it is indirect. The immediacy of our presence to ourselves keeps that presence from becoming the object of our thought. We can never separate our knowing selves from ourselves in a manner allowing the *act* of our knowing to become its own object. A knowing subject is always different from and beyond any object it knows — even when it tries to make its act the object of its knowledge. Having to know ourselves as subjects differently from the way we know objects, we know ourselves to be different from objects.

As subjects we are sources of spontaneous activity, called to live with other subjects in responsible, communal life. The history of humankind is largely a history of failure in that attempt, but the failure does not invalidate the necessity of the project. In fact, the failure can be accounted for in terms of the goal: human subjects are called to live with each other for the free, responsible agents they are, but, for reasons of their own, ambition and their lust for power and domination make them treat others — and frequently themselves — as objects to be externally controlled rather than as subjects to be respected.

To the extent that we recognize our difference from objects and become aware of the internal spontaneity of our lives as freely willing subjects, we become aware of our need for a special source beyond us from whom our subjective lives come. Our spontaneity, although genuine, is nevertheless conditioned and limited. Within our awareness of the limited agency we exercise, we become aware of our dependence upon — and so our affinity with — a self-sufficient agent not subject to our limitations. Only as we see the life we will as originating in the willing act of a self-sufficient agent beyond us does our willing of ourselves make sense.

Our immediate awareness of ourselves as living subjects furnishes us with a datum that must be respected and honored in its own right, for our activities as willing subjects cannot be derived from the physical, objective activity we study in the universe. The objective processes of the physical universe cannot explain the subjective agency of our lives.

Our awareness of ourselves as subjects leads to the awareness of a reality beyond us that escapes all objective determination and description. It is in our most immediate awareness of the spontaneity constituting us as the singular persons we are that we become aware of a willing presence beyond us enabling us — through the freedom of a gift bestowed — to be what we are. Recognizing an act of will beyond us — God's will — to be the only sufficient source of the willing we are, and so recognizing God as the only sufficient explanation of the uniqueness of our being in the world, there is no other alternative available to us but to acknowledge that God — *our* source — is the source of *all* that is. There is no other way *we* can understand the world.

It is within our experience of our willing activity as persons that we recognize the presence of a personal God beyond us, enabling us to be ourselves through the act of his will. It is only in the exercise of our living activity that we discover the living God; that God, because he is a subject who can never become an object, cannot be discovered in an objective analysis of the physical universe. It is not impossible for an objective analysis of the universe to lead to the conclusion that some objective existence greater than the world is necessary for the world to exist, but once such objective inference begins, the process knows no end. Each such object continually leads to another object beyond it, if physical explanation is the game one starts to play. The only beginning for which no antecedent, necessitating cause can reasonably be demanded — and so the only absolute beginning *we* know — is an act of free will. Only if the universe results from such an act can there be any *final* explanation of its existence. The bit of freedom we exercise, no matter how limited by physical restraint in the world at large and by physical correlation to the brains and nervous systems of our bodies, can be rationally explained only as the gift of a free act of will originating beyond us but taking effect within us. So it is that Christians believe in a creating God.

For Christians, all the pieces we need are now on the board, and the game of life can begin in earnest. It may appear to some that so much energy was spent getting the pieces on the board that there is little energy left for the game itself. Some may say that a game taking so much preparation is not worth playing. The only response I can offer to justify the lengthy preparation we have made is that some who say they want to play the game of life as Christians have spent most of their lives playing other games requiring different skills and attitudes. There are a lot of substitutes on the market. The other games are easier to play; they use different pieces, and they employ different strategies, but their reward for victory is different also.

The intrinsic nature of the contest for which we are now ready is not as difficult as the length of the introduction would indicate; as I have suggested, the previous training of players is the problem. Someone spending a lifetime lifting weights cannot justly use his or her muscle-bound condition as the reason to condemn high jumping. Similarly, a person who has spent a lifetime objectifying himself or herself in the search for objective success in the eyes of the world might be expected to have difficulty when asked to enter the "subjective" world that he or she previously denied altogether or at least condemned as unimportant.

The "pieces" required for "the game of life" we are playing are not acquired by effort; they are obtained by acceptance. Success in life requires that we accept reality, but we must accept reality for all that it is. Acceptance should not be difficult, and one would think it would be an easy attitude to adopt, but what is easy in itself can be difficult for those whose previous success was based on denial. For such people, it is difficult to "let go" and recognize everything that presents itself.

Much of the effort expended thus far has been intended to help us let go of habits and attitudes that keep us from acknowledging the fullness of the human world in which we live. Many people are strangers to their real selves, for their busy lives keep them from becoming aware of the spontaneous depths of their lives as responsible, willing subjects. What is given, the data with which we start, are the most important elements of any activity, for they determine what the activity will be. We can't sew with a broom, and we can't write music with a football. No one would think of beginning either activity with the equipment mentioned. But there are some games that can be begun before its players discover that necessary pieces are missing; it is possible to be well into a game of solitaire, for example, before realizing that a card is missing. Unfortunately, life is such a game; in fact, it is one game people may play to the end without realizing all the resources they have missed. As difficult as the game of life may be, if we play with a full deck of cards, we may at least find that there is hope for victory.

We should not push our metaphor of game-playing too far. Card games such as bridge are games played according to stated rules shared by all; a competent player can know all the rules ahead of time, so whatever happens in a given game happens within boundaries well marked and understood. It is reasonable to call life a game, and what happens to us in our lives can be referred to as the cards we have been dealt, but, unlike a game of bridge, in the game of life, after the cards we must play have been dealt to us, we find — as play continues — that we do not know all the rules. Unexpected, disrupting events occur, and our plans for a grand slam fail for reasons that ought to be against the rules. No player can master the game of life; sooner or later death will trump everyone's ace.

How are *we* to *get through life?* We now know something about ourselves. We know something about the world. And we have discovered the living God in the living of our lives. Discovering God's presence in our lives should be the greatest resource we have to enable us to get through life. In the end, our relation with God must be the key to successful living, but in the beginning the recognition of a God who wills creation into existence causes all kinds of problems. To say that the only absolute beginning of the universe meaningful to us is an act of free will is to say that everything which exists in creation depends upon that will. Christians believe that God did not have to create anything. When he did create, however, he expressed himself purposefully in his creation, for an act of will is an act of personal expression. It is the way a person's being is expressed in a specific situation. God's being is without parts or division, so whatever God does he obviously does in a wholly intended manner. For someone who believes in a creating God, there is no alternative to finding the ultimate meaning of creation in God's purpose for it.

The difficulty is that the wholeness of God does not seem to be found in his creation. Life in the world is filled with contrary tensions, which are bad enough, but millions of people have lived — and died — under what may appropriately be called the bondage of contradiction. In the twentieth century alone, millions of innocent people have been killed in death camps in Germany, Russia, China, and other countries of the Far East and Africa; millions more were killed in wars involving all the major continents of the world; still more millions have died and continue to die in drought-stricken lands and through other natural catastrophes. Poverty and violence grow in all of the major cities of the world, and bureaucratic government continues to demonstrate its inability to deal with the systemic inequities upon which it lives. No one who claims to believe in the Christian God can fail to have problems in the face of such events.

The magnitude of evil known in our world had not been reached in Paul's day, but many of the same kinds of evil we experience today were experienced then. No one has stressed more than Paul the necessity and sufficiency of faith; after his conversion, he realized and lived a total dependence on God in such a new and grateful manner that he thought of himself as having undergone nothing less than a new creation. He felt he had been reborn to a new life. But Paul, in agreement with the long-standing tradition of the Jewish people, acknowledged that not only his new life but everything in the world depended completely upon God. Belief in one God makes that God somehow responsible for everything in the world.

Paul recognized problems that had the same elements as the problems we recognize. Unable to solve such problems from his perspective of them, Paul found his way through them by switching the emphasis from the presence of the problems to the perspective from which he viewed them. Paul's responsibility was to keep his integrity by honestly admitting the problems he experienced to be problems; God's ultimate responsibility was greater than Paul's, however, for God was the enabling source of the problems Paul had only to recognize and admit. While it was true that God's responsibility was greater than Paul's, it is also true that God had greater resources and a different perspective on things than Paul. That difference was Paul's way through the dilemma. Thus Paul wrote to the Romans, "Who indeed are you, a human being, to argue with God? Will what is molded say to the one who molds it, 'Why have you made me like this?'" (Rom.

9:20). A short time later in the same letter Paul holds fast both horns of the dilemma when he writes of God, "How unsearchable are his judgments and how inscrutable his ways! For who has known the mind of the Lord? Or who has been his counselor? Or who has given a gift to him, to receive a gift in return? For from him and through him and to him are all things. To him be the glory forever. Amen" (Rom. 11:33-36). Paul echoes the words of Isaiah: "Who has directed the spirit of the Lord, or as his counselor has instructed him? Whom did he consult for his enlightenment, and who taught him the path of justice? Who taught him knowledge, and showed him the way of understanding? . . . Have you not known? Have you not heard? The Lord is the everlasting God, the Creator of the ends of the earth. He does not faint or grow weary; his understanding is unsearchable" (Isa. 40:13-14, 28).

I have remarked on the importance of the starting point — of what is given — for all of our activities. The equipment we are given and the materials with which we are furnished determine what we can do. Accepting life in the world for what it is should furnish a common starting point for all human beings. By virtue of living in one world, all human beings are related in their sharing of common problems. The question for us today is whether or not, in the light of those problems and of our growing knowledge of the universe, it is reasonable — that is, possible — to believe in an all-powerful, loving, creating, and redeeming God. Do prayers for the sick, such as those we prayed for our son, make sense? Can we make Paul's life of faith our own without either falsifying reality as a whole or denying parts of it?

The attempt to reconcile the existence of pain and evil in the world with the existence of an almighty, loving, and creating God has given rise to a special study called theodicy, after the coinage of Gottfried Leibniz in the early eighteenth century. Its technical name apart, the problem caused by the existence of evil in a world which obviously contains much that is good is one of the oldest difficulties to have perplexed humankind.

Once we are in the world, there is no alternative to accepting what goes on in the world, but, if we are not free to avoid all the pitfalls of worldly living, we can at least exercise our freedom in the manner in which we accept them. We may complain; we may protest; we may deny the value of protesting; or we may struggle to discover some overreaching context of meaning that allows us to include both the good and the evil within it. There is no alternative to the latter attempt for one who believes in a single and all-powerful creating God.

There have been those who believed in several gods, one good and one evil, and there have been those who accepted the arbitrary rule of fate, as in ancient Greece, to which even the gods were subject. Such alternatives are obviously impossible for Christians. It must not be thought that the tendency toward dual explanation is something restricted only to past history, however, for it lingers today in such contentions as Frohock's remark, which we earlier noted, that spiritual therapy and conventional therapy involve two incompatible realities. That statement can mean either of two things: it can mean that since the two therapies are incompatible, only one can be true; or it can mean that there are two incompatible ways of doing the same thing. For Christians, once again, neither alternative will do. To believe in two separate and conflicting realities, the spiritual and the physical, at the same time one believes in a single, creating God is surreptitiously to import the difficulties of relating several gods to each other into the life of the one God. Those who believe in one God must somehow see the polarity of good and evil as aspects of one reality rather than as two totally incompatible realities. Whether belief in one God can bear that strain is the question.

Theodicy, as I mentioned, is the attempt to find a reasonable — that is to say, a noncontradictory — way of reconciling a good

[58]

God with the existence of evil. In less worshipful and poetic terms than those of Paul and Isaiah, it has been pointed out that a truly satisfactory theodicy is impossible by definition. Theodicy is the attempt to explain God's mind to the human mind. It is the attempt to justify God to us. If one believes in God, it is not difficult to see that a successful theodicy requires a role reversal between God and us. It is impossible — to the point of absurdity — to try to reconcile God to human beings. It is not impossible, on the other hand, for God to reconcile human beings to himself by means that look absurd to human beings. A truly religious Christian accepts the apparent absurdity of the second alternative to be precisely what shows the need for human reconciliation to God. God's way of love appears absurd to us!

Even though we admit that, by definition, we can never know the mind of God, we cannot deny the needs of our own minds. Christian faith is not mindless faith. If we cannot escape the bondage of contradiction in the world, we cannot escape the meaninglessness of our lives. There are many dimensions of reality, and there are different dimensions of understanding. Somewhere among them all there must be some consistent, hopeful path of life that not only saves but also perfects and completes the dependent spontaneity of our willing selves.

Persons are wholes; creation is a whole; and the wholeness of God shows in them both. No one can deny conflict and tension in the world, but the conflict caused by contradiction is different from the tension found among contraries. Contradiction occurs when one thing is absolutely denied by another. "A" absolutely excludes "non A," for example: sound is totally different from nonsound, silence. Contraries oppose each other but not in the absolute manner of contradictories. Green and red are contrary colors; they exclude each other to the extent that they are different from each other, but they have something in common because both are colors.

The basic human need for meaning in our lives can be met

if we can discover an all-inclusive framework or context within which what appear to be the contradictions we face in the world can be seen as contraries. If it is possible to find a meaningful way in which to see the conflicts we face in our lives as aspects of one reality rather than as instances of the isolation and total opposition of two different realities, we may find sufficient strength in one pole of reality to get through the difficulties caused by the other pole.

We need help in order to live our lives in the world successfully. Many of our problems begin in the fact that we are embodied persons living in a world of bodies, and sometimes that world treats us — and sometimes we treat each other — as if we were nothing but bodies. To be in the world but not to be totally of the world is once again seen to be a good description of the human condition. We really are our bodies, but we are not just our bodies. Is there any way we can feel totally at home in such a world? Is there any way we can freely and fully embrace our lives in such a world?

I believe there is such a way. If we can live in a world in which God belongs, we can live in that world as one in which we belong — for our most basic affinity as persons, as willing subjects, is with God. If we can experience God living with us in our world, we can live in that world because it is God's world. Such living is not a theory; it is an activity in which our engagement must be our lives themselves. That activity is the only truly Christian theodicy.

Our task is to discern and to accept God's presence in the world, and it is to this task we must now turn our further attention.

6

What Can We Know of God?

IT IS impossible, by definition, for a created mind clearly to understand the mind of God. The human attempt to justify clearly the existence of a loving and all-powerful God with the evil we experience in his creation is just such an attempt. We cannot ask God's questions of ourselves; we cannot supply answers that can come only from God; but we also cannot help asking our questions about God of ourselves. Although our minds cannot equal the mind of God, we believe it to be God's will that we have minds, and so we believe it to be God's will that we use them. Once again it is a matter of perspective: we must remember that we can know reality only from our point of view.

As I indicated in the last chapter, the best we may hope for in our attempt to reconcile the existence of God with evil is to discover some perspective that enables us to understand — or at least live through — the disruptions we experience in the world as if they are contraries to the good they disrupt rather than absolute contradictions of that good. It is often a difficult task, and there are times when it seems impossible; at least it is impossible in our understanding of things. But our ability to believe in a single creating God depends upon untying the knot of the contradiction of good by evil. If we cannot do it ourselves, it must be done for us, but it must be done. Something beyond the apparent contradiction of good by evil must be found that, holding both good and evil in a common perspective, can furnish a resource for our lives beyond the conflict we experience in our lives. Such a resource is the creative act of God; God's creative action alone can supply the overriding context of meaning within which the significance of our lives is not lost.

Whatever exists exists by the permission and will of God. The conflicts we experience in life all stand within God's presence, and, because God is the unlimited source of creation, there is no doubt that God's resources exceed the resources of the restricted activities that define our problems. Because God made the world, the world is encompassed in his presence. That statement follows by definition from the fact of God's being the world's creator, but, as happens with all truths that "follow by definition," we get only verbal help from them in our lives.

Granting the truth that God is creator, it follows that God's work is present to him, but those of us who are in the world get no help in locating or recognizing God's presence in the world from that statement. It is too general. Our problems are located and specific, and only help that is as located and specific as our problems are will help us with them. An abstract statement, because it is abstract, is literally "out of this world."

We know that God transcends the world; the question is whether God is also in the world with us, and, if so, how he is in the world. Where can we locate him, and how can we call upon him? By contrast, we are sure that evil is in the world; evil is not difficult to locate. Our question about evil is the source of its presence.

Here, as Gilbert and Sullivan would have their befuddled characters sing, is a pretty kettle of fish. We know where God comes from in the sense of having good reason to affirm the unconditioned spontaneity of his life beyond the world; our difficulty is recognizing his presence in the world. The problem is reversed with evil: we recognize its presence in the world only too well; the trouble is that we do not see where it can come from if the universe is God's creation.

Theodicy is the attempt to account for evil's presence in the world in a manner that does not contradict God's nature beyond the world. But that attempt tosses still another problem into the kettle. We can know how God is in the world and where evil comes from only if we have some working idea of what God is like in himself. Theodicy's attempt to exonerate God against the charges of being either unjust or unloving can succeed only to the extent that God can be known to be one kind of God rather than another. Our ability to protect God from false charges depends upon our ability to know God as well as we know the charges. But to claim such knowledge is fraught with danger, no matter how high and noble our purpose may be.

We must start our defense of God, as we must start all of our activities, with what we know best. In this instance it is the inconsistent existence of good and evil in the world that we know best — not God. Starting from that inconsistency and on the basis of it, it is the task of God's defenders to rise to a consistent understanding of God that will account for the inconsistency found in God's creation. It is a big job for the clay to mold the potter.

And lest we think that the kettle is filled to capacity because of the number of complications caused by the tension between good and evil, let us not forget the tension between theory and practice. Theodicy attempts to reach a rational understanding of the tension between good and evil in the presence of God; its hope is to produce a theory that will give us the minimal understanding necessary to live meaningful lives in the midst of worldly conflict and disappointment. A good theory is always one that can be put to use and so make a helpful contribution to our lives. But the folk-wisdom contrast between theory and practice — that is, the contrast between what people say and what they do — is based on the common experience that theory does not automatically lead to practice. Many people who seem to be best at theory are found to be worst at practice. The search for an adequate theory may even become the means for preventing practice ever coming about. We can, for example, spend so much time trying to perfect a theory that we have no time left to use it. Such delay is an especially attractive temptation in the case before us.

We meet pain, sickness, sin, chance, accident, calamity, and death in the events of our lives. They are dimensions of reality that we must live through; they are not just ideas in our minds about which we can spend our time forming theories. Sickness, accident, or death may enter our lives before we have theorized about them, or they may interrupt our theorizing about them. Actually facing death presents us with a different reality than thinking about death in general.

We all know the difference between theory and practice; what is less recognized is the source of the distinction. The difference is based upon something that is by now very familiar to us: the distinction between a subject and an object. Practice involves us in the wholeness of our lives as subjective agents, while theory involves us in the objective analysis of a process that lies beyond the person as subject. When theories about death and accidents are held before us as objects of our thought, we are separated from them in our subjective lives; on the other hand, when we actually face death or are in an accident, there is no such separation. Both the nature of the problem and the resources for solving the problem are different in the two cases. We think about death and we actually face death in two totally different ways, and "totally" is to be taken literally in that statement. The resources available to our thought alone are not the same as the resources available to us in the wholeness of our lives as acting subjects. In the spontaneity of living, people often find themselves doing things they did not *think* they could do. Lifting up the front end of a car to free a child who is pinned beneath it or courageously fighting a disease against overwhelming odds are not uncommon examples.

Even when we finally come up with a theory that looks good, the theory alone does nothing for us. Our lives are not our theories. That is why there are times when the action of life — even if not perfectly understood in theory — offers us more than does a perfected theory about action. Responding to a person in need expresses an integrity of life that no theory of why we ought to respond to those in need can supply. Recognizing the difference between preaching and doing is perhaps the one common insight shared by every religion in the world. As living persons, we are essentially agents — living is something we do — and for that reason our essential fulfillment as persons is always found in our doing, rather than just in our thinking.

It is not my intention to proceed now with a discussion of something about which I have admitted we can have no knowledge — God's interior nature. God will always remain a mystery to us, for God infinitely exceeds our human capacities. God is Mystery. God is completely beyond us in his wholeness. There are not some parts of God we can understand and other parts we cannot. There is no aspect of God we can better understand than another, for God's absolute perfection makes it impossible for us to divide him up and get to know him, as it were, bit by bit. What may be called "growth in the knowledge of God" or "getting to know God better" refers more to the manner in which we increasingly and freely will to do God's will — and so increasingly live more closely with God — than it means increasingly having clearer ideas about God. We must never forget that God is subject-who-can-never-become-an-object.

Questions about how God is in the world and how we can live with him are still legitimate, however, and although we can make no claim to know God as God knows himself, we do have an awareness of him. That awareness is a kind of knowledge; it is just that we must never mistake the knowledge for what it cannot be. It is in the spontaneity of our lives as acting subjects that we recognize the unconditioned spontaneity of the living God. Our affinity with God is found in our active, responsible lives as agents. Whatever our awareness of God, and whatever our lives with God become, we must never, in our search for clarity, allow the categories of our thought to reduce God to something less than he is.

When we recognize our dependence on an unconditioned spontaneity beyond us, we recognize at the same time that we are creatures and that God is creator. We are *of* God, but we are not God. Awareness that we are *of* God is a way of knowing God, but it is an awareness able to be itself only within the spontaneous activity of our lives; it cannot be itself in the distilled categories of our thought.

Christians believe that God is life and that God is love; both are activities. Anything claimed to be known about God that is less than or different from the self-sufficient action of love is not significant knowledge of the true God. Consequently, where God is concerned, our knowledge arises more from concretely doing God's will than it does from abstractly thinking about God; we can relate to the action of God's life only in the action of our lives. Knowledge of the living God simply cannot be separated from life with God. There is nothing irrational in that contention, for the foundation of all reasonableness in religion is to be related to the only God there is, the living God, not anything less.

Knowing the will of God to be the source of the spontaneity with which we will ourselves, we still wonder how to relate God's creative will to the totality of our lives in the world. We continue to come back to the troublesome triad of God, good, and evil. How can we reconcile all three? The most obvious way, of course, is to argue that the three terms are not absolute in the same sense. One can argue that God and goodness are absolute in a manner that evil is not. Evil may then be seen to be an indirect by-product of something else that is willed, rather than being directly willed by God. The procedure is a time-honored course to take, and it is so honored because it has a basis in fact. In such a complex system of systems as the universe, systems that are positive in themselves indirectly produce negative effects when they intersect. Disease offers a common illustration: there is nothing wrong with bacteriological growth in itself — in fact, it is a good — but when such growth takes place within the differently organized growth of an organism, the conflict in growth patterns is called a disease in the host organism. The comparison is similar to different sections of an orchestra playing different melodies at the same time: the combination produces dissonance.

Another way of trying to untie the knot of good being opposed by evil in creation, in a manner that absolves God from responsibility for the problem, is to say that there are some things even God cannot control. This, too, is a time-honored approach, and its understanding of God has held sway in Western Christendom for centuries. The course of the argument will no doubt sound familiar to those with even a casual knowledge of theology.

In the understanding of God we are now considering, God is described as necessary being. God, as Keith Ward puts it, is the one and only "being that cannot fail to be, that possesses its essential properties by necessity." As self-existent, unconditioned being, Ward explains, "God must have a given nature. What is unique about it is that it alone is what it is by absolute, unconditional necessity. There is no sense in complaining about the Divine nature, once one sees it to be absolutely necessary (I take this to be the teaching of the Book of Job). No being, not even

God, can properly be held responsible for what it is, or what it causes or wills, of necessity."[1]

Knowing himself, God knows the full perfection of being, and in that knowledge God knows all the worlds he could create. Those worlds are part of God's nature, so they necessarily are what they are. Because of God's self-sufficient perfection, he does not need to create anything, but, if he chooses to create, he has no choice about the intrinsic structure of the different worlds from among which he must choose. Evil and suffering are necessary aspects of some of the worlds that God could choose to create, so, if he chooses one of those worlds, evil and suffering will necessarily be found within it. God has no choice after his initial selection, for he has to choose among the alternatives that his necessary being presents to him.

God cannot be held responsible for what he has no control over, so God's exoneration from the charge of injustice appears to be well on its way. But God cannot yet be fully acquitted, for it may still be asked why he chooses to create a world with suffering when he could just as well have chosen a world without suffering. One defense of God maintains that this world, for all of its pain and suffering, might nevertheless be the best of all possible worlds. A perfect God, so the argument would go, would choose to create nothing less than the most perfect world possible, so, this being the world we got, we may rest assured that it is the best world possible. God is unable to create anything better.

It is not difficult to see that such a conclusion would be only a rhetorical victory for God. The claim of victory would once again be based on a position that "follows by definition" — if God is perfect, his creation must be as perfect as possible. There is no real help in that assertion as we take our chances in the world.

1. Ward, *Divine Action* (San Francisco: Harper San Francisco, 1990), pp. 18, 27.

There is another reason, however, why such a victory for God would be an apparent victory only. Upon consideration, "the best of all possible worlds" is found to be a self-contradictory description. There is no way to choose such a world. The variety of values contained in the unlimited number of worlds God could create are so varied that no single criterion can be found by means of which anyone, not even God, could say that one world is absolutely better than all the rest. How many dimensions should the absolutely best world have — two, three, four, or more? Should it be fully formed or evolving? Should it have different species of creatures? How many? What kind? Should the richness of free will but the possibility of disobedience be allowed? Should it have music or not? Should it be only physical, only spiritual, or a combination of both? For all of the wisdom available to God in his self-knowledge, any world God would choose to create would still appear to be an arbitrary choice.

The understanding of God as being-in-itself, as the being-which-must-be, is deeply ingrained in Christianity, particularly in Western Christianity. The view was conceived and given birth by Aristotle and baptized and confirmed by Saint Thomas Aquinas. To demonstrate the reasonableness of Christian faith in his *Summa Theologiae,* Aquinas proceeded by showing that beings which need not be — contingent beings such as we — can reasonably be understood only if a being that cannot not be — a necessary being — exists to account for them. By the use of natural reason alone, Aquinas maintained, it is possible to prove the existence of one supreme cause which is the first cause of everything else that exists. The first thing known about God, then, is that God is the one being that must be.

Having proved the oneness and the existence of God, Aquinas held that our knowledge of God's trinitarian nature results from God's self-revelation. Since necessary being contains all the perfection of being within it, and since personhood is a perfection of being, we may conclude, by our reason alone, that God is personal. God's all-perfect being must include personal perfection in its fullness or God could not have created persons. Because we are able to know and prove that much by our unaided natural reason, the reasonableness of God revealing his personal nature more fully to the persons he created provides a philosophical apology for the propriety of Christian revelation, even though the content of the revelation goes beyond the capacity of human demonstration. Human beings are able to receive from God more than they can prove for themselves about God.

While human reason cannot prove the truth of what God freely reveals about himself, human reason can disprove a doctrine's claim to be a revealed truth if the doctrine can be shown either to be internally self-contradictory or to contradict natural truths. Nowhere, neither in the natural order nor in the supernatural order, does truth contradict itself. The oneness of the God who is Truth shows in the oneness of truth. Thus, revelation, although not positively able to be proved by human reason, does have to meet a standard of reasonableness that can be checked by human reason.

In the theological system we have been sketching, God is admitted to be personal because personhood is a perfection of being and God is the fullness of being. Necessary being is God's basic nature, and within that nature personhood, like every other perfection of being, is located. When God's nature is so conceived, *being* is prior to *person* in God; the impersonal necessity of God's being is prior to the loving freedom of God's life. Precisely that understanding of God has been generally accepted in the West, and has been used for centuries as a criterion to judge the truth or falsity of other doctrines claimed to be revealed by God.

Whether such use is justified, however, may be questioned. We may well ask whether or not the uniqueness of personal life can be fully explained in terms of impersonal being. Can the uniqueness of Christian revelation be judged by the categories of a generalized philosophy of being?

There is reasonable cause for concern. Keith Ward, whom I have chosen as a contemporary representative of the position I have been summarizing, writes, "If part of Divine perfection is love, then a God who loves and wishes to unite creatures to himself must actually do something to show his love and effect that unity, within history."[2] That statement well presents the structuring of Christian revelation by the categories of being. The statement implies that, since God's essence is necessary being, love is something that must be found within it; that being the case, it is most reasonable that God would reveal his love to his creatures by some free, special act in history. Hence the life of Jesus Christ.

A rational context has been provided within which God's free and loving revelation of himself can occur. But it may be asked whether it is the fully Christian God who can reveal himself in such a setting. Can it be true to say of the Christian God that *part* of his divine perfection is love? Christians believe, as the First Letter of John says, that "God *is* love" (4:16, italics added). God is not just partly love. Jesus' words, recounted in John's Gospel, that he *is* "the truth, and the life" also apply directly to God (14:6). God's love is the first thing one meets in meeting the Christian God; love is not just one characteristic among others that is deduced from some more basic characteristic of God.

It is one thing to say that God is necessary being, and it is another thing to say that his being is necessary. "Necessary" in the first statement refers to the necessity of our being having a source beyond it to account for it; such a source is absolutely necessary if our being is to be reasonable. "Necessary" in the second statement refers to the internal nature of God's being. I have repeatedly said

2. Ibid., p. 190.

that we, as creatures, cannot know God in himself, and I must not appear now to deny that fact by writing about God as if we knew what his intimate life is like. On the other hand, since we are *of* God and have an awareness of his presence in our lives, we must respect that awareness for what it is. We must keep that awareness as free from contaminating elements as we can.

I have said that the awareness we have of God is a kind of knowledge, and I have said that we must not make the knowledge something it is not in the search for clarity in our thinking about God. We can know things only from our point of view, but it is the *things* we wish to know. Our sensory perception and intellectual cognition have been compared to a light we project into nature in our search for knowledge. We can know of nature only what the light we project brings into view — and we must be aware of the limited perspective we are therefore able to have — but it is still nature that reveals itself in our light. The situation is not dissimilar in our knowledge of God.

We recognize God — and our affinity with God — in the action of our lives as conscious agents; it is in the spontaneity of that action that our awareness of God arises. While it remains true that we cannot know God as God is in himself, we can know the uniqueness of our encounter with him, within which we recognize his presence. Falling short of knowing God as God knows himself, we can at least protect the living encounter we have with God from imported, foreign elements that would intrude upon it and reduce it to something other than itself. Knowing God in the spontaneity with which we will ourselves, we know God as the spontaneously willing source of ourselves. We know God in his free gift of ourselves to ourselves; that is, we know him in his enabling us to be ourselves. Any claimed knowledge of God that would put a limit on his spontaneous freedom would destroy his self-sufficiency and thereby make him something less than fully personal.

Love is a free act or it is nothing. If God is love, as Christian faith maintains, there can be no necessitating constraint — either within God or outside God — to the personal freedom whose exercise is God's loving life. We obviously cannot clearly conceive the God about whom we are speaking. The unease we experience as a result of our limited capacities will constantly tempt us to clarify our thought by projecting our nature and our concepts into God's life. It is difficult to let God be God, but if we are able to keep from replacing his nature with ours in our thinking of him, we may find the salvation God offers us to be a gift liberating us beyond anything we could clearly conceive. We may then know the new life in Christ that Paul wrote about by experiencing the new birth he experienced, and we may then know in our lives the peace he wrote about, the peace that surpasses all understanding (Phil. 4:7).

Two "models" of God are now before us: in one, as we have seen Ward put it, God is thought of as necessary being that "possesses its essential properties by necessity"; in the other view, God is totally free, spontaneous act because God *is* love. Love is a personal act of will; for that reason the will of God is primarily stressed in the second view. The first view stresses God's knowledge, that is, the knowledge God necessarily has of what he necessarily is — and about which he has no choice. That knowledge, over which God has no control, specifies what God can and cannot will.

Austin Farrer advocates our regarding God as Unconditioned Will. On that basis, Farrer goes on to say that God "is all he wills to be, and wills to be all he is: for his act is himself, and his act is free."[3] Keith Ward criticizes that position by saying it "is misleading, since it can suggest that God might will himself to

3. Farrer, *Faith and Speculation* (New York: New York University Press, 1967), p. 118.

be absolutely anything. But it makes no sense to speak of God as 'pure will,' without any given, antecedent nature. Such a will would be wholly contentless and arbitrary. God must have a given nature."[4] Farrer's position, which stresses the primacy of God's will, is called "voluntarist," while Ward's position, which stresses the intellectual stability of God's being, may be called "rationalist." Is love, an act of will, or knowledge, an act of reason, primary in God?

To be able to ask which of two things is primary in God should be a warning to us that our thinking is already getting offtrack. There is no such thing in God as a faculty of will that can be separated from God's faculty of reason. Conflict over the primacy of reason or will reached an all-time high in subtlety in the Middle Ages, when Thomists and Franciscans vehemently argued with each other about the relative superiority of cherubim and seraphim — the former were said to be lost in the contemplation of God's truth, while the latter were transported in the love of God.

God's spontaneous life of love includes, from our point of view, what we call both willing and thinking. Those who, like Farrer, stress God's unconditioned will and freedom appear to make God irrational and arbitrary from the point of view of those such as Ward. On the other hand, in the opinion of Farrer and others, to say that God has a nature given to him and a set of ideas over which he has no control destroys the self-sufficiency and wholly personal nature of God. It makes God's personal life subservient to impersonal being.

Christians believe that human beings can know God only to the extent that God reveals himself to them. Because God is a subject who can never be an object, objective analysis, as I have tried to show, can never give us significant knowledge of God. It

4. Ibid., p. 27. The last sentence has been quoted earlier.

is in the attempt to remain true to that insight that Farrer refers to God primarily as will. For Farrer, "free will" is a way of referring to a personal subject's responsible activity in the activity's totality. So taken, free will is simply the way an acting person is himself or herself in responsible action he or she undertakes. The freedom of our expression is limited in the world and conditioned by factors external to it, but that is not the case with God.

To say that God's freedom, if unrestrained, would make his actions arbitrary and would allow him to will himself out of existence or otherwise contradict himself is no argument against unconditional freedom. God's freedom is not an act of will separated from God's person or reason. God's unconditioned freedom is one with his unconditioned personal life. As the fullness of personal perfection, nothing God is, does, or wills is unreasonable. No opposition is found between reason and will in God as may be found in human beings. We must recall again that there are no separate faculties in God. And even when such separate terms as *reason* and *will* are used of God, it must be said, as Irenaeus said when writing against heretics in the second century, that God does not first think and then will. God wills what he thinks and thinks what he wills. God is a perfectly spontaneous living subject unmixed with anything else.

The statements we are making challenge our usual habits of thought, but a God who would not so challenge us would not be God. To say that God is love is to say that the act of love is God's act of existence. God does not first exist and then begin to love. Similarly, it cannot properly be argued, as it was by the Scholastics, that the existing God can first be shown to be one and that then, within that oneness, God can be shown to be personal. The oneness of God is the oneness of a person; neither aspect — personhood or oneness — can be separated from the other. As best our minds can fathom, it is truer to say of the Christian God that God exists because he is personal than to say that he is personal because he exists. There is no existence of or in God that is impersonal. When Christians say God *is* love, they are actually saying love is a person.

There is no such thing as an unspecified act of existence; existence is always of one kind or another. Christians believe that the self-sufficient source from which the existence of all dependent beings comes is a personal act of love. True freedom is unconditioned freedom; it can be nothing less than itself, which means that it cannot be subordinate to anything beyond itself. Love is a free act, and it follows from that fact that it is as true to say that God's freedom entails his existence as it is to say that God's love entails his existence. God exists because he loves, because he freely wills himself. So understood, it is not nonsense to say that God freely wills his existence! The meaning of the statement is that there is no existence of God that can be separated from his love and free will.

God's freedom is truly creative in his own life. This freedom is not a hollow attribute defined in purely negative terms alone. That is to say, God is not free just in the negative sense that there is nothing outside him that can oppose him and prevent him from being himself. God's freedom, so defined, would be freedom by default. The freedom of God's life is significant in the positive activity constituting his life. Thanks to God's revelation of himself, Christians know the creative freedom God exercises in his own life to be the eternal generation of the Son and the eternal spiration of the Spirit by the Father in the life of the Trinity.

For Christian faith, nothing is prior in reality to loving personal presence. The one thing that the impersonal vocabulary of being can neither describe nor explain is *gift*. The objective vocabularies of science and of a philosophy of being can describe the processes of the physical world; they can adequately deal with physical interactions and mathematical inference. But the free, meaningful offering of a gift by one person to another totally escapes the objective representation of a physical process. The free offering of a gift, arising from no necessitating antecedent conditions, cannot be reduced to a physical process, although physical processes are the vehicles by means of which gifts are given in the world.

Gifts are a source of meaning to those who receive them, and gifts are given with meaning by those who offer them. It is no accident that the most personally meaningful acts in our lives are accompanied by gifts. We give rings at engagements and weddings; we give presents on birthdays; we give dinners and parties to celebrate significant events in our lives. The significance of a gift originates in the free act of the person who offers it. A gift is the way a person, in the spontaneous freedom of his or her deepest self, gives himself or herself to another person as that person is a spontaneous, free self.

The offering of a gift is the most meaningful statement one person can make to another person. If we were able to see the world in which we live and our lives in that world as gifts from God, we would have the context of hope necessary to live our lives meaningfully in the world.

We have found reason to accept God as the source of the world. We have said that the opposition of good and evil we experience in the world is found within God's presence. We must now go on to discover how God offers the gift of himself to us in our lives. It is in the context of gift that our lives find their highest meaning. If God does give himself to us and live with us in the world, I contend that we can live in this world as a world in which we feel we belong — no matter what happens.

7

God's Will and the Way Things Are

IN THE Judeo-Christian tradition, God's presence is a gift that God makes of himself to his people.

It is impossible to argue to — or to infer — the proper name of a person. Proper names are *given* names; they are generally the names that parents give their children. The names given to us for the special persons we are arise from the spontaneity of free choice; thus there is no way those names can be inferred from our later actions or characteristics. No one gives God's name to God, of course, but, being eminently personal, God has a name — a name known to him alone. If God wishes, as an intimately personal act, he can reveal his name to others. Such personal self-revelation grounds the faith of Christians and Jews.

After Moses' encounter with God in the burning bush, in which God tells Moses to return to his people and tell them that the God of their fathers will lead them out of their slavery in Egypt, Moses asks God what he should say to the Israelites when they ask the name of the God who sends him. God, as is well known, tells Moses that his name is I AM WHO I AM, or I

WILL BE WHAT I WILL BE (Exod. 3:14). In the incident, God is indicating that he comes to be with his people for whom he, God, is; God comes to be available to his chosen, to be present with them, and to do something for them.

The uniqueness and specialness of God's willed presence for the deliverance of his people are signified by God's revealing his unique and proper name as the one who is present. God declares his will for his people and his concern for them in the gift of his personal name to them. He who will be what he will be declares that he wills to be with his people to lead them out of their misery in Egypt (Exod. 3:17). The presence of God makes a difference. Christians see the ultimate presence of God with his people in the life of Jesus, and so it is that Jesus, in his prayer to the Father recorded in John's Gospel, says, "I have made your name known to those whom you gave me from the world" (17:6).

A gift is an act of will. Creation is a free act of God's will, so creation is a gift. God's presence with his people for their deliverance from Egypt through his servant Moses, and, even more fully and intimately, God's presence with his people for their deliverance from sin and death in God's only begotten Son, Jesus the Christ, are gifts God makes of himself in which he reveals his nature with special clarity. On the other hand, when we consider God's creation as a whole to be a gift, the ambiguities, tensions, and even contradictions about which we have spoken seem to belie the love God reveals himself to be in the special gifts of his presence. We find ourselves again confronting the opposition of good and evil in the world, and we find the opposition to be within God's presence to his creation.

Living in the interconnected web of activity we know as the universe, we cannot, in the perspective we are developing, live in the world as if it were an assemblage of things and events within which we can seek God's will only in specific and isolated instances. For us, to live in the interconnected web of activity known as the universe means that we live in the interconnected web of God's willed intentions. In that sense, to live in the world is to live in God. When we live this way, we find God's presence everywhere; no location is empty of God's will. God is as fully present in the world as he is said to be in pantheism, but God is not simply identified with the world as God is in that doctrine. God's will is everywhere in the world, but God's will is not exhausted by the world.

In the view I am presenting, we do not search for God's will only here and there in the world as if the rest of the world had nothing to do with his will. It is not a matter of trying to discern God's will among energy patterns and subatomic particles in which God's will is absent; the activity of the energy patterns and subatomic particles that science studies is itself the will of God. At that basic level of physical reality, as Austin Farrer contends, God's will is best discerned by the descriptions that science is able to make of the activity and energy it studies.

The basic dynamism and structure of energy studied by the physical sciences are the will of God for that level of reality; they could not exist without God willing them. But God's ultimate will for creation is not revealed at that level of his creation. At least we human beings can detect no discernible purpose at that level other than the interconnectedness of the activity we discover in its parts and in the way they work together as a whole. God works through self-acting agents in the world; God creates things to be themselves — which is what "being a world" means — and then works through the agents as themselves. Some of the agents are free and some are not, but all are respected for what they are. All too frequently, believers in God try to separate themselves out from creation as a whole in their search for meaning instead of including themselves in the totality of God's willed intentions.

I have said that whether one is an atheist or a believer, all human lives begin in the same world. Our personal views of the world are, to be sure, part of our world, and, from the point of view of personal meaning, we can say that, although people live on the one planet, Earth, they live in different worlds on that planet. But the oneness of the planet and of the physical system and subsystems of the planet's life supplies a common point of origin for the activities of all the earth's inhabitants. Granted that the tension and the opposition of good and evil about which we have been speaking expose all of the earth's inhabitants to common dangers, disruptions, and disappointments, there are only two ways that such brute facts can be accounted for: either they arise from "sheer, unconditioned choice" by God, or they arise from impersonal necessity within God.[1] It is possible to shrug one's shoulders and do the best one can espousing either of the two alternatives I have mentioned, but I hope to show that "the best one can" allowed by the first alternative is very different from that allowed by the second alternative. In either alternative, whatever happens happens through things being themselves, identities that God respects by being the one who made them themselves.

The presence of God in the unlimited freedom of his will is the source and meaning of life. The closeness of God in the total gratuity of God's will is Job's consolation in the midst of the unjust suffering he endures. The meaning of the book of Job is quite the opposite of the meaning that Keith Ward ascribes to it. The teaching of the book of Job is not that, once we see God's nature to be determined by absolute necessity, there is no sense

1. Austin Farrer, *Faith and Speculation* (New York: New York University Press, 1967), p. 117.

in complaining about God; the teaching of Job is that God is himself in his totally unlimited freedom, and that we miss the living God if we try to understand him and circumscribe him by our ideas and expectations.

Job's three friends are all theologians who explain to Job why his suffering is just. Job suffers, they say, because he has sinned. Their understanding of God and of God's justice is complete, systematic, and airtight. To Job's claim that he suffers innocently and unjustly, they reply that God is incapable of such unjust action. Job can suffer only because he has sinned, and if Job does not recognize his sin, the difficulty is in his moral sensitivity or memory rather than in God's justice. The reasonable view is that God punishes evil and rewards good in the world. The difficulty is, as we all see so frequently, that God does not meet the expectations of human justice in the world.

In the face of that dilemma, Job does not conclude that God's being is so dictated by necessity that God is helpless to order things differently; instead, Job discovers the presence of God in his life in a new way. After the last of Job's friends speaks, God speaks to Job, saying,

> "Who is this that darkens counsel by words
>   without knowledge?"

(38:2)

God then goes on to state his independence and freedom in creation by asking,

> "Where were you when I laid the foundation of the earth?
> Tell me, if you have understanding.
> Who determined its measurements — surely you know!
> Or who stretched the line upon it?"

(38:4-5)

God next details the creatures he has made — the stars, the sea, the clouds, snow, hail, rain, thunder, lightning, the lions in their dens, deer, ravens — asking in each instance whether anyone told God what to do. The illustration loses almost all force for people of our day, but God then goes on to tell Job that his (God's) freedom is mirrored in the freedom of wild beasts that human beings are not able to control. God says,

> "Who has let the wild ass go free? Who has loosed the bonds
>   of the swift ass. . . .
> It scorns the tumult of the city; it does not hear the shouts
>   of the driver.
> It ranges the mountains as its pasture, and it searches
>   after every green thing.
> Is the wild ox willing to serve you? Will it spend the night
>   at your crib?
> Can you tie it in the furrow with ropes, or will it harrow
>   the valleys after you? . . .
> Do you have faith in it that it will return, and bring your
>   grain to your threshing floor?"
>   (39:5, 7-10, 12)

Human desires are no harness to God.

After God asks Job if a faultfinder can contend with the Almighty, and after God unleashes another long list of the events of nature over which Job has no control, Job answers God:

> "I know that you can do all things, and that
>   no purpose of yours can be thwarted."
>   (42:2)

In the experience of God's living presence, Job discovers that human concepts of justice and the conclusions drawn by the human mind about God completely miss God. Realizing that he had previously uttered what he did not understand, Job declares,

> "I had heard of you by the hearing of the ear,
> but now my eye sees you. . . ."

(42:5)

Job contrasts the distant knowledge about God that comes by hearing with the intimacy of direct personal presence with God, which he compares to seeing God. The supposed knowledge of God that came by hearing was the explanation of God offered to Job by his friends, but knowledge by hearing also refers to Job's own attempt to understand God conceptually. The knowledge that comes by hearing refers to all conceptual, objective knowledge about God; it is different from the way we know God in the immediate experience of his presence. Job's discovery is that, in the immediate presence of God, he is so enlivened by the free and gratuitous act of God's will to be with him — he was so embraced by God's love of him — that he recognizes that the staticness and objectivity of human thought about God amount to missing the true God altogether.

The hard lesson Job learned was that God did not create the world to meet human expectations and to allow human beings to replace God as creation's meaning givers. Life's meaning and fulfillment are found only in the gratuity of God's gift of himself to us. Our freedom responds to God's freedom, but God's ability is not limited by our reason.

The completeness of Job's submission to God's unlimited freedom in the intimate presence of God is so total that the final result of the book of Job can appear to be one of absolute irrationalism. God can do anything he wants anywhere, anytime, and who is Job — or who are we — to question him? The freedom of God's will is so heavily stressed in the book of Job because the book wants to lead people to an experience of the living God rather than to a lifeless doctrine about God. And, as we have seen, the willing action of a person is the ultimate expression of a person's presence. In stressing God's ability to do anything he wills, we must not forget that the will of God is not an isolated faculty that can run wild and contradict either the reasonableness or the loving concern of God. A person's will is simply the whole person as a subject being itself, and, in an eminent manner, that is true of God also.

Our challenge in thinking about God is a challenge to see how personal a God we can stand. There is no denying that God is Mystery. But mystery, without losing its mysteriousness, can be of different kinds. The word *mystery* is used in the plural, and we speak of the mysteries of love, sex, science, and the past, to offer only a few examples. The truest mysteries are personal, and the ultimate Mystery is Person. The mystery of God can be focused, as it were, in either God's reason or God's will. We can ask either "Who knows the mind of God?" or "Who knows the will of God?"

If the mystery of God is primarily located in God's mind, as Ward contends, our conflicted experiences in the world and our unanswered questions about the opposition of good and evil must ultimately be attributed to the necessity of God's nature over which God himself has no control. In that view, although there is no external constraint upon God in the exercise of his will, there is internal constraint exercised by the immutable ideas contained in his being that God must necessarily accept. In his personal, willing expression, God is limited by impersonal ideas. In spite of God's independence and singularity, God exercises his will within a context over which he has no control. The Greeks thought the gods were subject to a fate beyond them; in the view we are discussing, the objective nature of the ideas in God's mind subjects God to an impersonal fate residing within him.

To locate the mystery of God in God's will is, as I have said, to maintain that nothing impersonal can be found within God. God is absolute Person, so there is no aspect of either his life or his being that is separable from the spontaneous, free act of the love that God reveals himself to be. Only such a God is the eminently personal God who infinitely transcends the limitations and conditions to which we are subject in our personal lives. The best our limited minds can say is that God is so completely personal that, in him, willing and the context of willing coincide. God is the pure act of personal spontaneity limited by nothing either within or outside of himself. God is genuine Source of all through and through.

For Christians, it is more consistent to say that God wills all things — some for reasons we cannot understand — than to say that there are some things God cannot will and has no control over. If we see the mystery of God's will everywhere, there is hope everywhere. Truly personal living is then possible everywhere.

We need the immediacy of God's presence everywhere, but we must never fail to ask ourselves whether or not we are ready for God's presence everywhere.

Presence is a difficult thing to write about or to speak about. Its immediacy and pervasiveness — its global nature — renders it incapable of being captured in, or demonstrated by, any particular experiment. Personal presence cannot be reduced to an objective element among the objects of the world. Presence manifests itself in particular ways that we can recognize, but it cannot be penetrated in an isolated, crucial experiment. Personal presence is not made up of parts. Its "core," because it is the spontaneous activity of a subject, always transcends its physical expression and can never be exhausted by physical expression.

Apprehending the divine presence in the world literally makes a new world, for God's presence is always creative. God's presence is the lively spontaneity of God's will constantly bringing newness of life with it. The divine will is present in the course and existence of the whole of creation and must be acknowledged in that totality. God's presence can never be found if it is looked for as if it were a singular, different kind of divine thing among the other things in the world. God's presence is always taken on the whole in the whole, for, as I have said, personal presence always overflows any given, particular expression it may employ.

Personal presence manifests itself in the purposeful nature of its action. Purpose is the means by which presence is itself, but personal presence cannot be reduced to its purposes. Presence is better defined as the origin and enjoyment of purpose. Purpose is the vehicle of presence. It is because presence cannot be reduced to purpose, even though presence expresses itself through purpose, that there is no single experiment or combination of experiments that can decisively prove or disprove the purposeful presence of God in the world. Purposes, arising from the spontaneous activity of subjects, have the same transcendent relation to objects that subjects have. An unknown purpose behind a known purpose is always possible.

The impossibility of experimentally proving the presence of God in the world should not surprise us, for we have much the same problem in trying experimentally to prove our personal presence to each other in the world. From the very beginning of our lives, we live our lives as persons within our presence to each other. We do not first clearly know ourselves and then experimentally try to make our knowledge of others as clear as that we have of ourselves. In our earliest days of infancy, we know other people — mother and father or their surrogates — before, and better than, we know ourselves. Our first knowledge of ourselves, and so the source of our self-esteem, is primarily dependent upon the way other people relate to us and treat us before we are conscious of ourselves. Our lives in the presence of each other as persons are the roots from which our lives as subjects develop;

later to set ourselves the task of objectively trying to prove the presence of other people in the world is like trying to treat the roots of a tree as if they were no more than pieces of fruit that had fallen from its branches.

We are rooted and grounded in the will of God, and we live our fullest lives when we freely will God's will. There is no alternative to our living in each other's presence, and there is no alternative to our living in God's presence. The first recognition of God in our lives is the recognition that we have always lived in God's presence. Whenever we discover God, we discover the God who has already been present with us. God is the source of newness in life, but we can never discover a God who is a novelty. God is God, I have said, because his presence always makes a difference; the basic difference that God makes to us is the gift of us to ourselves — his gift of the act of spontaneity that separates us from nonexistence in our creation.

Because of our free will and because we live our bodily lives in a world of bodies, it is possible for us to deny God by living as if we were only bodies, or to deny him by consciously opposing him with our free wills. The first kind of denial is the adoption of a "minimalist view of reality"; the second type of denial is called sin. Life that we acknowledge living in the presence of God is the life most natural to us, for our nature as persons comes from God. But if God is turned into something he is not — a big, threatening object beyond us — life with him is seen to be most unnatural. And why not?

Neither atheism nor theism can be proven absolutely by our reason, which is to say that problems in the world remain to be explained whichever view one adopts. Taken on the whole, granting the difficulties in the world that must be admitted by both atheists and theists, it is more reasonable — and by far more natural — to confront those problems in the presence of the God who is Source of all, rather than to say that ultimate reality is an impersonal surdity and that both we and our problems are, at bottom, meaningless accidents.

But we are not left to make our ultimate decisions about the meaning of life on the basis of nothing more secure than a philosophical decision "based on the whole." A God who is only probable is no God at all. Traditional Western theology is right in saying that God's being is necessary to explain our being. How we get to know the God who is necessary for us is the issue.

We have seen that a God who existed but made no difference to us would be no God at all. It is only within the spontaneity of God's will that the spontaneity of our wills makes sense. God did not create human beings by calling them into existence in accordance with an idea contained in his perfection, give them the faculty of reason, and then rest content knowing that, by their reason, they could discern his existence and basic nature. God takes the initiative both in giving creatures to themselves by creating them, and then in giving himself to them after creating them.

There are mysteries about the way God spoke to his people before what Christians and Jews take to be the special calling of the people Israel, but, as signified in God's metaphorical speaking to Adam, we can rest assured that, in a way he willed, God called all of Adam's descendants to him. The most primitive awareness of God that has been revealed by our study of antiquity was invariably a matter of personal relationship. God was never concluded to as an abstract philosophical principle. In our sophistication, we may call such early awareness of the divine presence naive and anthropomorphic, but it contains more truth than the concept that personal spontaneity can come from impersonal processes. Primitive human beings at least related to living gods!

It can be said that we necessarily live in the presence of God, but the necessity of our so living does not necessitate our recognizing the fact. The God who is the living spontaneity of love always seeks and elicits a personal relation with those of his creatures who can enter into such a relationship. Personal presence is a reciprocal relation, and we must believe that in the evolving course of history God has related to his people — all human beings — in a manner corresponding to their sensitivity and ability to discern his presence. For reasons that remain locked in God's will, some nations and peoples have evidenced more spiritual discernment than others in the long journey of human development.

Knowing God's will as it has been revealed to us, we believe that God in all times and in all places spoke to his people as they were able to hear him. Christians believe that all that went before was preparation for God's definitive speaking to his people through his Word, his only begotten Son, Jesus the Christ. In the life of Jesus, God entered the world in the ultimate fullness of his presence to human beings. As the letter to the Hebrews puts it, "Long ago God spoke to our ancestors in many and various ways by the prophets, but in these last days he has spoken to us by a Son, whom he appointed heir of all things, through whom he also created the worlds" (1:1-2). Writing to the Galatians, Paul said that "when the fullness of time had come, God sent his Son, born of a woman, born under the law, in order to redeem those who were under the law, so that they might receive adoption as children" (4:4-5). The Epistle to the Colossians, after warning its readers not to be captive to human thought and expectation, declared that in Christ "the whole fullness of deity dwells bodily" (2:9).

After the event of his resurrection, the whole sequence of the life, death, and resurrection of Jesus strained human expectation and comprehension to the bursting point. Jewish anticipation of the coming of the Messiah was ages old by the time of Jesus; the signs of the Messiah's coming had been foretold, and the preparation for his coming, through the keeping of the Law and the admonitions of the prophets, was well in hand. Actually, at the time, several different types of Messiah were anticipated in different areas and in different subcommunities of Judaism, one being a triumphal and regal Messiah, the other being a humble and suffering Messiah.

People were looking for the Messiah in Jesus' day. The expectations were all in place. But for those who accepted Jesus as the Messiah, the Christ, previous expectations were burst as well as fulfilled. The first Christians called Jesus the Christ because they recognized him, by his resurrection, to be the one they had awaited and expected; but he was also different from and much more than the preparations made for his coming anticipated. Instead of being the conclusion expected from preknown premises, he was the beginning of something radically new. Rather than the fitting conclusion of all that had gone before, life in him amounted to new birth into a spontaneity of loving that destroyed the old concept of perfection through Law. To live in Christ was to live a new freedom of the Spirit, a life knowing no measurable bounds or proportions; no longer could it be possible to feel secure about oneself and think everything necessary for salvation had been accomplished when definable duties had been carried out. Calculation could no longer serve as the means to personal righteousness.

What do Christians believe God has done in the life of Jesus?

In my attempt to describe the nature of personal presence, I distinguished the presence of a person from the events in which that presence is discerned. Personal presence may be recognized within events, but personal presence is not an event itself. Events take place within and are the vehicle for personal presence. Personal presence arising from the spontaneous depths of a living subject always transcends and overflows the limited particularity of a given event. That explains why, if we do not achieve our purpose one way, we will try another. If I can't reach you by phone, I'll write a letter; if he won't help me out because we're friends, I'll offer him money. We can persist in trying to accomplish our will by any number of different means. Certainly personal presence and the purposes originating from it are more than the physical processes we employ to express ourselves in the world.

The strain — and the release — that the life of Jesus brings to our human understanding is that, somehow, in the event of his life the presence of God *is* with us. Living in the presence of someone is an activity. Recognizing the presence of someone is something we do; it is different from reading about or thinking about someone. Personal presence is not a theory. We must be invited into someone's presence by an action originating in the person's presence.

Personal presence is concretely historical; it occurs at a certain time and place, and it involves the sharing of at least two persons' lives and wills. So God, who wants us to recognize his presence in our lives, and who wants us to live our lives in his presence, opens his presence to us in a historical activity that is of one kind with the activity of his presence. God invites us into his presence in the life of his Son in the world.

God, the subject-who-can-never-be-object, enters our world by giving himself a bodily location in our world of bodies. In the spontaneous gratuity of his will, God lives his will for us and with us in the life of Jesus. From the iife of Jesus on — and his life never ends! — we know what God's will is and how to will it. We have but freely to accept the gift of the Spirit, whose reception made Jesus the Christ, into our lives, and the inner spontaneity of Jesus' life becomes the inner spontaneity of our lives. In the gift of the Spirit of Christ to us, Jesus' inner disposition becomes our inner disposition; the meaning of Christ's life is given to our lives.

8

Some Problems Left Over

AT THE end of the month, we would rather have money left over than bills. As we get near the end of our reflections, we would rather have resources left over than problems. But some problems remain. We will look at them now, as the head of a household takes stock of remaining concerns at the end of the month, and, when we have considered everything, we may find some additional resources to handle whatever is left.

Based on our most immediate experience of ourselves and God's freely offered revelation of himself in Jesus Christ, we have been led to the acknowledgment that God creates us and the universe by a free act of his will. We have established that we live from and within God's presence, that God is concerned about us, and that God gives himself to us. It makes sense to pray to such a God — to share our concerns with him and to express the totality of our dependence upon him. It is not just reasonable that we should express ourselves to God, however; it is also reasonable for us to expect God to respond to us. Every truly personal relationship is reciprocal. Persons are spontaneous centers of activity, and the spontaneous source of responsible activity that every person is must become evident and be respected in all fully personal relationships, even — or especially — the relationship with God.

Where mutual respect and reciprocity are not found, a personal subject is being treated as an object, and such mistreatment, at least at the theoretical level, has been one of the major philosophical protests of the twentieth century. The God who is the source of our subjectivity will certainly not treat us like objects. If we pray to him, he will hear us, and hearing us he will respond to us. To pray without expectancy is not to pray. But can we expect all of our prayers to be answered? That question is a problem remaining for us. What can we say about prayer and the efficacy of prayer? These are not new problems; such questions have been asked in one form or another by people throughout the religious history of humankind. No one can be unconcerned about how calls for help are answered. We must now express our concern about that problem within the understanding of reality we have developed.

Being members of God's created universe, it is obvious that we pray to God from within the universe and that God must respond to us within the same context. As people have prayed to the gods — or to God — over the centuries, those seeking God's help have understood the world in which help is needed in many different ways. In early times, human beings exhibited a primitive, diffuse, inexplicit sense of awe and mystery at the forces surrounding them, over which they had no control; as time went on, human beings developed more precise ideas about how to conceive the external forces upon which they depended and how to react to them. Animists acknowledged living spirits who were worthy of worship, and to whom gratitude should be shown, in all living things. Local gods lived in areas that were especially important to primitive people — in rivers and springs, on mountaintops, and in the heavens. The presence of deities had no difficulty getting into the world in those days; such presence was discovered and acknowledged everywhere.

As the centuries advanced and human skills increased, nature became more and more an object for human beings to use, analyze, and manipulate. The forces of nature, rather than being manifestations of the subjective presence of spirits and gods, gradually became reduced to mechanical forces. Nature began to be studied and controlled by the impersonal language of mathematics, and experimental science became the model for truth. The empirical study of the objects of nature gave human beings unprecedented control of nature. In early atomic theory the fundamental constituents of reality were thought of as little objects out of which the big objects of our experience were made. Atomic structure was compared to the structure of a solar system, only on an infinitesimally smaller scale, with electrons orbiting the atomic nucleus like planets orbiting a sun. As some enthusiasts pushed the mechanistic understanding of reality, there was neither a place nor a need for God in the world. The Deists, as is well known, said that God was necessary to get the mechanistic system of the universe up and running, but, once that was done, the world had no more need of God, and God had nothing more to do with the world.

Today it is no longer possible to think of the atomic and subatomic worlds as miniature versions of the world of our everyday experience; physicists describe their deepest probings in mathematical equations that defy translation into sensual terms. They discover dynamics in the physical universe that cannot be discerned by sensory perception; in present-day physics, ordinary experience counts for nothing. Describing the forces of nature, physicists now employ a space-time matrix with eleven dimensions, adding at least seven unseen dimensions of space to our experiential three dimensions. In fact, according to relativity physics, forces are better described as patterns of space-time rather than as activities going on within a framework of empty space and time.

In the expanding universe that began between fifteen and eighteen billion years ago, physical science no longer conceives of the universe and our world within it as being made up of solid objects; instead, physical reality is thought of as a web of interconnected energy patterns. In earlier theories, when big things were thought to be made up of little things, the basic understanding of the universe came from studying the behavior of the subatomic particles of matter. Based on a mechanistic theory, such study was done by observing the duration, speed, and position of particles in their orbits.

When such measurement was done, however, it was discovered that the light directed on a particle to measure its position and velocity affected that particle. It turned out that the smallest amount of light that could be used to make a measurement, called a quantum, disturbed the particle to be observed by changing its velocity. What is now called the "quantum factor" showed that the mechanistic independence of the physical world was not as complete as had been previously supposed. Because there is no observation of subatomic particles that does not interfere with and so alter the state of the particle being observed, the personal subject who is the observer seems partially to "create" or determine what is observed just by observing it. One can secure information about either a particle's momentum or its position, but the very process of observation makes it impossible to know both.

All of this has changed how the physical universe is understood: it is now asserted that a degree of randomness is found at the deepest level of the universe's existence. The basic physical structure of the universe cannot be accounted for by a simple determinism. The most basic description of physical reality given by science is now stated in terms of probabilities rather than in terms of the precise measurement and description of isolated, individual entities. It is on this basis that the universe is understood to be not a collection of objects but an interconnected network of vibrating energy patterns. The action of observing subjects in the world makes a difference to the world, and the unity of the world has been discovered to be more tensed in its dynamism than a merely mechanical uniformity would allow. The universe is a whole that is more than its physical parts, and at the most basic level of physical reality, we discover interconnected probabilities rather than individuals that can be themselves in isolation from each other.

Modern physics still speaks of the laws of nature, but the laws are now statistical in form. Atomic events are intrinsically statistical, which means that a certain instability exists at the root of the physical world that allows, through minute fluctuations which cannot be individually predicted, a newness of the future that cannot be extrapolated from present knowledge. Radical newness is possible in the world; the future is not completely determined by past and present conditions. Laws of nature still exist, but they are better described as "general principles of organization" than as regulatory statutes that cannot be violated.

When taken in general, the various systems and subsystems that compose the universe have a unity and consistency upon which we can depend, yet, within that consistency, individual events occur that are not predetermined and that can, because of their action in an interconnected dynamic network, cause major changes elsewhere in the system. The slightest unexpected bump of one foundation card in a house of cards causes the destruction of the whole house. In such an interdependent system, everything within the system depends upon and affects everything else in the system. Thus the random movement of an electron to the right or the left can inject a new factor into physical reality that in time, because of the continuing reaction to the initial change that proceeds throughout the system, will produce a major difference in the course of the world. A cancer may be cured; a new species may evolve. Events originating at the quantum level of reality are able to change the course of nature in a radically new way while still remaining within the understood course of nature.

Such an understanding of the universe is an encouragement to those who believe in God and in the power of prayer, for it allows a place in the universe for God's will to be exercised freely without contradicting the nature of the universe as a whole. The undetermined probabilities lying at the foundation of physical reality allow God to "steer" the world by causing one, rather than another, of several possibilities to occur. In ways undetectable by us, God can intervene in the world for his purposes, and nothing is violated in our scientific description of the world. On the whole, everything remains the same; the balance we know as the physical universe is not tipped, but certain specific events occur the way they do because they, rather than alternative events, are God's direct will. Thus, while we can generally determine the course of a cancer and statistically estimate the life expectancy of a person at a certain stage of the disease, specific individuals, as a result of prayer, may defeat the odds and astound their doctors by an unexpected remission and even a cure. That was true of our son, Tony.

The general situation I am describing is not unusual in any statistical description of a population. Statistical projections about the length of human life and the frequency of illness determine our insurance rates. We are all aware that, while in a given population sample the average life span may be seventy-one years, some individuals will live much longer than that and others will die earlier. Such deviations may be accepted by some as mere physical variations that have no additional significance, while others may find purposeful, causal activity in the events about which the first group is unaware. Prayer and God's response to prayer are candidates for such activity.

To those who believe in God, it is helpful and encouraging to have the impartial descriptions of physical science provide a place for God to act in the world. As encouraging as such a place is to belief, however, belief in the efficacy of prayer does not arise from and does not depend upon scientific descriptions of the universe. The mathematical descriptions of nature are value neutral to belief in prayer, as is shown by the fact that the same mathematical descriptions can be differently interpreted by people of opposing views. Both we and the universe around us are more than our physical parts — there is an entitative structure and order to our lives and to the life of the universe that amount to more than the physical components of either — so materialistic descriptions alone will never furnish the ultimate basis for, or supply the ultimate answer to, our primary concerns as purposefully acting subjects.

We are still grateful for help wherever it may be found, and what I have said so far is helpful in enabling us to understand why, even when we believe prayer is efficacious, some prayers are answered according to the prayers' intention and others are not. Understanding the laws of nature to be general principles with a statistical component, we understand that exceptional things can happen to certain individuals without statistical averages being destroyed. We pray to God from within the world, and it is in the world that we ask for help. For the reasons I have offered, it is reasonable for God to be concerned about us and to offer special help to us, but all that within the given context of the world. Prayers that would destroy the nature of the world and the universe as a whole cannot reasonably be expected to bring the answer they intend. As is commonly pointed out, if all healing prayers for the sick were granted, and if everyone was saved from death by the prayers of loved ones, we would be living in an entirely different world than we do. We offer our prayers in the midst of a reality extending far beyond us that God has created, and we must not expect to live our lives with God as if God and we were the only reality that mattered.

Discovering an area in patterns of probability where God may act individually and not destroy the pattern as a whole is a way of fitting God's action into the system of nature. But we have seen that God does not express his will only in certain places that do not upset our calculations. Everything that exists does so within God's will by his will. Reality, as we know it, is God's will. In that sense, the system of nature "fits into God"; God does not have to fit himself into it.

God's will is found in the structure of the whole, and what we desire and request in prayer from our point of view must always be subject to the good of the whole as it has been chosen by God. Science is an accumulated body of knowledge put together from our point of view; it is an exercise in which we try to confirm our perspective on things. In religion we offer our perspective up to a perspective greater and more inclusive than ours that calls us to itself. Because of the different orientation of science and religion, it is obvious that neither activity can supply the principal foundation for the other, but that is only to say that we must not confuse one kind of thing with another. Rocks don't hatch in nests, and birds don't came from volcanic eruptions.

When we admit that God's perspective on things is different from ours and that it is his perspective which must prevail over ours, we get little specific help in understanding why individual events occur in the world as they do. A religious person may say that whatever happens ultimately happens for the best, but, just as we saw that "the best of all possible worlds" does not help us understand why this world rather than a different world exists — because there are so many different kinds of "best" — so we cannot see what is "best" about the catastrophes and destruction going on around us. In a universe as inclusive as ours, there is no single criterion by means of which we can judge — from our point of view — what the absolutely best is. When we also recognize that, among all the prayers offered to God, many are prayers requesting opposite effects, we realize that it is far beyond our ability to judge what ought and what ought not to happen in response to prayer. Democrats and Republicans and Independents pray for victory in the same election; Serbs and Croats pray for the defeat of each other; retired people pray for interest rates from their investments to go up, while young people trying to buy a house pray that rates will go down.

Earlier I said that to pray without expectancy is not to pray, and I went on to ask whether or not we can reasonably expect our prayers to be answered. A classical text for the advocacy and efficacy of prayer is found in the letter of James: "Are any among you suffering? They should pray. . . . Are any among you sick? They should call for the elders of the church and have them pray over them, anointing them with oil in the name of the Lord. The prayer of faith will save the sick, and the Lord will raise them up. . . . Therefore . . . pray for one another, so that you may be healed. The prayer of the righteous is powerful and effective" (5:13-16).

Taken as it stands, that statement is an oversimplification. Not everyone who is prayed for is cured, yet, though we acknowledge that fact, it is still reasonable to believe that prayer is powerful and effective. It may be observed that the translation of the passage I have just quoted states that prayer is to be used for healing: pray, the readers are told, "so that you may be healed." I have just said that not everyone prayed for is cured. Those who believe in faith healing or spiritual healing today generally make a distinction between healing and curing. To be cured means that physical well-being is restored: a disease or an incapacity is banished. "Healing," on the other hand, is a more inclusive concept. Healing may include a cure, but it may not. To be healed is to be restored to a wholeness of being that involves spiritual orientation, acceptance, and integration — and that may occur even if a disease is not cured.

The distinction between healing and curing is a valid and important one. Healing is a response to prayer that enables more prayers to be answered affirmatively than might appear at first sight. Healing is a reasonable expectation for *every* intercession for health. In the passage before us, the Greek verb that is translated "healed" does not make the distinction between healing and curing that I have just discussed. The verb generally means "to save," and the word "savior" comes from it. The intention of both "healing" and "curing" can be included in its meaning, but, since the passage states that the sick will be raised up by prayer, it seems clear that the meaning "cured" rather than "healed" is intended in here.

Given this interpretation, the statement in the letter of James that everyone prayed for is cured is an overstatement. But even the admission that it is an overstatement does not deny the power and effectiveness of prayer. Our spontaneous lives as persons are a gift to us from the spontaneous Source of all reality, God — we are our ourselves only from God and with God — and it is because of, and within, this relationship that we express our personal concerns to God. God made us persons to be with him. The only relations we have with God are personal relations, and because personal relations are always reciprocal and mutual, we must freely share our lives with God, as he shares his life with us.

Prayer to God arises out of our total dependence upon God, a totality of dependence we have shown our existence to be. We do not believe in God and pray to God because we have inferred, from the proven results of prayer, that God exists. We do not believe in God because of the results of prayer; we see the results of prayer because we believe in God. Because prayer is the relation of a subject to a subject, the significance of prayer can never be justified objectively. Prayer is not subject to scientific experiment, as Fred Frohock pointed out. Narrative rather than experimental repetition is the language of prayer, because prayer is born of personal relationship, and freely willed personal relationships have a singularity about them that cannot be generalized and reproduced for objective analysis. Faith can be confirmed in the course of objective events, but the objective description of events, by its very nature, cannot require faith.

Because my relationship with God transcends objects and arises from God as a subject calling me and giving himself to me as a subject, I pray to God with the certainty that I am being heard — and with the certainty that God will respond to me. My prayer arises out of a complete dependence on God that I live before I pray; thus God has nothing more to prove to me after I pray. My whole being is lived trust in God, and that trust, once in place, allows me to accept whatever events follow my prayer as contained within God's will for ultimate good. Once we recognize God with the total dependence of our being, we need do nothing more to admit that we are not God, and that God's will, found in the whole of reality, deserves precedence over our will in the particular situations in which we find ourselves.

Acknowledging God's will in the whole of reality is something we find difficult to do. The sheer magnitude of the subject overwhelms us. Large numbers can be written with precision and calculations using them can be exactly expressed, but when it comes to absorbing their significance in our lives, we are lost. Astronomers tell us that there are approximately one hundred billion galaxies. Each galaxy has about a hundred billion stars, and an equal number of planets may additionally be found in each galaxy. Galactic distances expressed in light-years and the multiplication of suns and possible planets like our earth outstrip our senses and imaginations, even though the entities referred to are familiar to us. On the one hand, the sheer magnitude of physical reality shrinks the importance of our planet and of our lives in the cosmic scheme of things; on the other hand, the chemical elements and atomic structure with which we are familiar in our world are found to be the same as those in the farthest reaches of the universe. The scientific understanding of our world is the key to our understanding of galaxies that are hundreds of billions of light-years away from us. As personal subjects, we are also members of the created universe, and so our knowledge of ourselves is also a key to our knowledge of the whole universe extending beyond us.

No matter how overwhelmed we are by the magnitude of physical reality, we have no alternative but to live our lives for what they are, respecting our experience and our self-identity as the only means we have of understanding the farthest reaches of reality beyond us.

In the course of our everyday lives, people sometimes say, when discussing prayer, "Why should I pray? God has so much else to do. Why should he be concerned about me? How can he be concerned about me? Major events in my life are minor events in the world; to presume to elevate my concerns to God's attention reveals an immature grasp of reality and should be embarrassing."

Complications arising from life on our planet alone are enough to make us wonder how God could have any "time" for us in the major events of our lives — sickness, war, death — let alone in lesser matters like interest rates and buying houses. The opposing prayers of people should offer complications enough for a full-time deity, but when we add to that, as we have done, that God's will is the source and sustaining power of everything that exists, our limited orientation to reality is totally lost. Imagine God directly willing the movement of one electron to the right rather than to the left, while God is at the same time willing the existence of hundreds of billions of galaxies containing so many electrons that we couldn't even write down the number of them in a billion lifetimes. We simply wouldn't have the time to record the number of zeros required.

If we're going to have a problem, we might as well have it for all it's worth. There's no point in letting the problems of sustaining and guiding the different atomic, molecular, cellular, organic, personal, and social activities of this world trouble us about the reasonableness of praying to God. Let us place the problem where it belongs — in the total reality of the universe and in the myriad activities going on within it. When dealing with God, we need to have our problems "writ as large as possible." God should be our ultimate concern — and that ought obviously to require our problems about God to be our ultimate problems. There is no sense in holding back. Nothing should benumb us more than God's difference from us; that is why we do better worshiping God than trying to compete with him.

I have tried to emphasize the problem many people have with prayer — whether God can or will be concerned about us and the concerns in our lives, when there is so much else for God to do — to help us appreciate, as fully as possible, the solution we are able to give to the problem. Because God is the Source of all reality, I have frequently referred to God's transcending his creation. God's transcendence of creation is the difference of his being from the being of the creation he freely wills. We live from God's will and in God's will, but we are not God. Because we and the universe in which we live do not need to exist, because our being is a limited and dependent being, our being and the existence of the universe are called finite being. We depend on something and someone beyond us.

We say that God's existence is infinite because it is completely self-sufficient, depending on nothing beyond itself. Nothing limits it within or outside of itself. The self-sufficient spontaneity of God's love is infinitely beyond anything we can conceive or approach. And that is the point! The infinity of God infinitely exceeds the finite. As overwhelmingly big as the universe is to us, there is no ratio between it and God. There is no ratio between the finite and the infinite. Finite creatures such as we cannot get closer to God by degrees, understanding God better and better as we go along, until there is less and less of God that is mysterious to us. God is total Mystery, and there are not some things about him we can understand and other things we cannot.

If we acknowledge the completeness of God's difference from us — the difference that makes God God — we will not import the limitations of our lives into God's life. Our not seeing how God can will everything he wills and how God keeps everything going that he keeps going, while at the same time leading creation toward a perfection beyond itself, is simply the way we realize that we are not God. It is to encounter God's radical difference from us. It is our consolation that God is able to do what God is in fact doing. To deny the consolation because we cannot understand God is to deny our natures as creatures who are totally dependent upon God; it is to be dissatisfied with the fact that we are not God.

If God really is the Source of all beginnings, no questions can be asked about how he is himself. There is nothing prior to God that can explain God. That is why God is God. Praying to such a God is the only God worth praying to. And when we pray to such a God, we can submit our wills to his, knowing that, in the end, as in the beginning, God's will is all in all.

9

The Final Solution

IN THE previous chapter we looked at the problems remaining, which in itself points to the fact that no view — atheistic or theistic — can clearly explain why reality is as it is. There are always problems left over, questions we cannot answer.

We do not see how all things work together for good, if for no other reason than we are not in a position to see all things. Located as we are in place and time, we understand that we cannot understand everything. Knowing there is much we do not know at least leaves open the possibility for the ultimate triumph of good over evil beyond our knowledge, even though the struggles going on around us seem inconclusive — or discouraging. Accepting the limitations of our knowledge, we can salvage something that might be called a negative consolation. Since we cannot conclusively prove that things do not work together for the best, we cannot deny with certainty that all things do work together for the best. Still, if we are going to be ourselves, we need more help than that.

Everything we have dealt with in these reflections has obviously been dealt with from the human point of view. No other alternative is available. We have been discussing problems *we* have and difficulties *we* experience in our lives. We have difficulties that are objective and real, but we have also seen that we are subjects. As subjects, we live spontaneous lives that cannot account for themselves, and, with the immediacy and certainty with which we can know ourselves, we — if we know ourselves — recognize that we come from a spontaneously loving Source beyond us from whom and within whose presence we become ourselves.

The universe is a system of systems and subsystems of active events. Our lives, like the universe as a whole, are chains of interdependent events. The basic factor of reality is action, which, although it can be verbally described, cannot be reduced to the static forms or abstract formulas that describe it. Personal presence is the activity we have found most basic to reality, for a free act of will is the only action we know that is truly originative.

The physical and biological sciences have gone a long way in describing how the physical universe evolved, but, in addition to knowing how the universe developed, we also want to know why the universe exists. Science discovers patterns of change in the expanding universe. But, as physicist Stephen Hawking asks, why should there be a universe at all? Science can write descriptions, but why should there be anything to describe? Why did the universe spring from one kind of initial state rather than another? Equations need "fire," as Hawking — following Pascal — puts it, something different from them, in order to put them to use and make them significant.

As I have said so many times, the only source ultimately meaningful to us that can explain why reality takes one form rather than another is a spontaneous act of will. Recognizing a personally free Source of reality, we recognize the Source and Goal of the meaning of the universe and of our lives in the universe. But that knowledge and certitude about creation as a whole does not give us the ability to see God's purpose clearly in many of the individual events of our lives.

In the absence of knowledge that is God's alone and that can never be ours, how, as I asked at the beginning of these reflections, are we to get through life? How can we be ourselves — that is, live with hope — in the face of the disregard and destruction of human life that we experience in the world? Millions of men, women, and children were herded together like cattle and slaughtered during the Holocaust. Rape, pillage, and murder run rampant in Bosnia; famine and disease stalk the Sudan; crack babies are born in New York and in all of our larger metropolitan areas; the HIV virus is being spread throughout the world by deceitful and ignorant personal behavior; institutional injustice promotes inadequate health care, education, and job opportunities. Multitudes suffer and fight disease in their personal lives, but society at large also shows signs of ill health. The sickness of society and the illness of an individual are different in kind, but the basic elements of the human condition are found in each.

The physical illness of an individual is not the same as the illness of society, in which, for example, impersonal institutions rob people of their future, deny their past, and fail to understand their problems in the present. But whether people will be treated as subjects or objects is a question immediately relevant to every problem we can mention, individual or social. The human condition is the context of every human reality, whether it be individual or social, positive or negative. The significance of human existence is found — or questioned — in science, art, literature, and music, just as it is in environmental pollution, ethnic cleansing, the selling of drugs, and political hypocrisy.

All the problems I have mentioned arise from events that intersect the chain of events constituting our lives. We must respond to and live through the challenge with which we are presented. Street crime in the inner city may be no more than a topic of conversation in the suburbs; if crime is kept far enough in the distance, it may not even be thought about. But when a suburban woman's car is carjacked at the shopping mall, or your mother has a heart attack, or I have a mysterious fever, we find ourselves involved at the action level of reality to which the action of our lives — not just our thoughts — must respond. The real problems of our lives are those demanding our response with the same fullness of reality presented by the problems. Recently I called on a young priest in the hospital who had cancer, and who had made numerous sick calls himself. He said to me, "It's a lot different having cancer than talking about it, believe me." The events of our lives are different from the words we or other people use to describe our lives. When our lives are attacked, we must respond with our lives, not just our words.

Both individuals and communities need strength to live and act in the world with hope. But where is hope to come from? It must have the same degree of reality as our problems, or it will be no help at all. Hope must have the reality that the events of our lives have, or it cannot enter our lives. Hope must arise from something actual that happens, or it will be no match for the events that threaten us by their actuality. A real problem needs an equally real solution.

Reality is always some kind of action. What is the ultimate activity founding all reality? It is responsible, personal action originating in a free, purposeful act of will. Willful personal presence is the beginning and the end of all reality. How are we to get through life? By recognizing the Source and Goal of our lives to be the self-sufficient personal presence of God freely willing us into existence, so that we may freely will God's will as our ultimate fulfillment. We cannot know as God knows, but we can will God's will for us, and that willing is our life. Free gift, not nature, is both the source and the perfection of our life.

In the last chapter, I said that if we're going to have a problem, we should have it for all it's worth. Prudent planning should always be done using a worst-case scenario. If we can find a way through the worst thing that can happen, we know we can handle lesser matters. I have tried honestly to admit that specific events arise in the world that challenge the existence of an all-powerful and loving God. God does not directly will evil, but we cannot understand how God can even permit much of the evil we see in the world. To see innocents suffering, as one does in the halls of a children's hospital, should test anyone's faith in a loving God.

In discussing the problems people have with prayer, one problem I mentioned was that many of us feel that God is too busy doing other things in the world to be concerned about us. If we stop to think about it, there is a reasonableness to such a problem; but, if we stop to think about it, the problem is bigger than it might at first appear. God is busy with much more than our world. God wills the universe in its entirety. So, as I said, if we're going to have a problem, let's have all of it, and think about the significance of our prayers when they are located among the millions of galaxies in the universe, not just the events on earth. The reason I wanted to emphasize the bigger problem rather than minimize it is this: it is only by giving it the greatest possible emphasis that we can be led to a realization of the infinitude of God's difference from us. God is God because he is totally different from us, and any way in which we try to compromise God's difference in order better to understand him results in our dealing with a product of our own rather than with God.

To believe in God but not to be able to understand why things happen as they do is not a new problem. I should think that no believing person could go through life without having this problem; the inconceivable thing would be for a person who believes in God to have no such problem! In the Judeo-Christian tradition, the situation is certainly not new. The biblical books of Job and Ecclesiastes speak directly to it. Both books have given voice to the anguish and the deepest experience of people over the centuries who have endured suffering they could not understand.

Neither Job nor Ecclesiastes could be accused of not confronting the real issue of the incomprehensibility of unjust suffering and of the inability of human thought to penetrate the ultimate mysteries of human existence. Both Job and the Teacher of Ecclesiastes are dumbfounded conceptually. Job's friends try to offer explanations for his suffering, but they are of no help. Job is finally offered the solution to the puzzle of how to get through the incomprehensible suffering he is experiencing: his recognition of the presence of God in his life. When Job recognizes God's immediate presence to him, he is given a new and different resource for the problems he endures. In seeing God, Job is engulfed by a reality so different from human expectation that he is lifted out of the human perspective. When Job lives in the immediacy of God's presence — when Job sees God rather than just hearing about God — Job lives *with* someone rather than living *for* something. The intensity of God's life, which is the activity of God's willed presence, becomes more real to Job than the presence of his torment. It is a case of gift overcoming nature.

The book of Ecclesiastes begins, "The words of the Teacher, the son of David, king in Jerusalem. Vanity of vanities, says the Teacher, vanity of vanities! All is vanity. . . . I, the Teacher, when king over Israel in Jerusalem, applied my mind to seek and to search out by wisdom all that is done under heaven; it is an unhappy business that God has given to human beings to be busy with. I saw all the deeds that are done under the sun; and see, all is vanity and a chasing after wind" (1:1-12, 12-14).

After struggling to acquire as much wisdom as he could, the Teacher "perceived that this also is but a chasing after wind" (1:17). To say that all is vanity is Ecclesiastes' way of saying that, whatever its appearance, everything human may be compared to smoke. Human achievement is vaporous and passes away with no trace. Everything changes. Nothing human lasts, for in the end death contradicts human life.

The Teacher of Ecclesiastes is so violent in his expression that a first reading of the book may give the impression that it is a statement of absolute skepticism and despair. In fact, the Teacher emphasizes the smoke-like and transitory nature of everything human only to heighten the contrast of God's reality to it. In this way, there is a basic kinship between Ecclesiastes and Job. For all of his condemnatory and skeptical language, the Teacher believes in God, but the God he believes in is so different from us — and so mysterious — that God cannot become a part of, or be used in, human calculations. The Teacher is convinced of the presence of God in the world, but he also realizes that we do not know God as we know the objects of the world, and that our knowledge of God cannot be used as we use our knowledge about the world.

The Teacher also stresses the absolute difference of God from us. Even to think we know God on the basis of our experience is to preconceive and to presume what God will do in the future. But such preconception is vanity; it denies God's total difference from us and God's absolute freedom to be himself. It is the witness of Ecclesiastes, as it is of Job, that the smallest single presumption about God totally removes us from God's presence. For the Teacher and for Job, true wisdom is not a body of knowledge absolutizing the human point of view; true wisdom is complete dependence upon God acknowledged by never thinking we are God.

The reality of the presence of God and of the freedom of God — more accurately put, the reality of God's presence in his freedom — is the highlight of both Job and Ecclesiastes. When we see God, when God's presence encompasses our lives, God's wholeness and integrity overwhelm the instability we are. In God's presence, our brokenness is replaced by his wholeness. Human reality is subsumed in divine reality; we are lifted beyond ourselves, and our brokenness is healed in the action.

All of that is said in the Old Testament books of Job and

Ecclesiastes. God is understood to be a redeeming and liberating God in the Old Testament. In Psalm 102 (as found in the Book of Common Prayer) we read,

> For the Lord looked down from his holy place on high;
>   from the heavens he beheld the earth;
> That he might hear the groan of the captive;
>   and set free those condemned to die.
>
> (vv. 19-20)

Thus God looked down upon Job from above. In Jesus, on the other hand, Christians see God groaning with us within our world. In what is often referred to as "Jesus' abandonment on the cross," we find the ultimate subsumption of human reason into Mystery beyond itself. It is significant that, in his feeling of abandonment, Jesus cries out "Why?" to the very God he cannot see. By crying out to the Father through his feeling of abandonment by the Father, Jesus turns the absence of reasonableness into a new mode of being with God. One mode of being becomes the occasion of another mode. What appears to be the contradiction of God's presence becomes a new way to be with God; absence of reasonable expectation acknowledges the presence of God's difference.

In discussing the relation of an artist to his or her work, Gustave Flaubert wrote to George Sand that the artist's presence, like God's, should be felt everywhere but never be seen. Flaubert went on to ask whether God ever expressed his opinion. By stressing God's difference from us in his absolute freedom, it might appear that I, like Flaubert, am arguing that God's presence is everywhere, but that God, since his will is found in all things, has never expressed an opinion of his own that would commit him to one side rather than another in the conflict going on between good and evil in the world. As Christians we believe that

God has done more than express an opinion: we believe that God has specifically and unequivocally revealed himself and his purpose in creation in his Son, Jesus Christ, the Word of God made flesh.

As Christians we believe that God has spoken to us in a Word that reveals God's absolute freedom. For when Christians believe Jesus to be the Word of God, they do not think the Word that God has spoken is just one word from among a number of words that God could have chosen to speak. The Word that was made flesh was not an objective word over which the Father had no control. The Word is the Father's free expression of himself. The Word is nothing but the expression of the Father's love; that is why the Word — and so the Son who is the Word — controls nothing in his own right. The Son can do only the Father's will, for the Word whose expression the Son is is nothing but the Father's will. As Hans Urs von Balthasar has put it, it is precisely the selflessness of the Son that reveals the Father's self.

God is love, the giving of oneself to others. Jesus came into the world not to express an opinion about God or to be an expression of God's opinion; Jesus came to do and to be the will of God in the world. Jesus is God's will as that will is a human event. Nothing is more characteristic of the life of Jesus than the prayer he offered at the Mount of Olives: "Father, if you are willing, remove this cup from me; yet, not my will but yours be done" (Luke 22:42). To accept Jesus as God's Word made flesh is to accept the fact that our relation to God is always an action, a living, not a set of ideas. Christ himself tells those who assume his name as Christians that "not everyone who says to me, 'Lord, Lord,' will enter the kingdom of heaven, but only the one who does the will of my Father in heaven" (Matt. 7:21).

Personal presence is an action, and we can live in the presence of God only with the action of our lives. Because God is creator, his will is found in everything that exists, or it would not exist.

But it is at the level of creation in general that the difficulties we have been discussing arise; it is within God's creation that we feel threatened and in which we are attacked. I said at the beginning of this chapter that, if we are reasonably to live lives of hope, we must have more to go on than the negative consolation that the final triumph of good over evil cannot be disproved. If God, in the spontaneity of his love, loves us and always makes the first move toward us, he should do better than leaving us to find consolation in what we are not able to disprove.

It is because God, in his love, does not leave us to find what consolation we can in life by ourselves that "in these last days he has spoken to us by a Son, whom he appointed heir of all things, through whom he also created the worlds" (Heb. 1:2). God's loving provision of the help we need is indicated in those words from the letter to the Hebrews, for in them the God who comes to redeem and save human beings in Jesus Christ is identified with the God who created human beings and heaven and earth in the first place. The source of human hope in the world arises from the fact that the creating God is not different from the redeeming God! The God who redeems us is the God who created us, which means that, in the life and presence of Jesus Christ among us, we see the purpose of creation and God's will for his people.

The Word that God speaks among us in his redeeming Son is the very Word through whom the universe was called into existence. In the life of God's only begotten Son, Jesus, God identifies himself with his creation as well as bringing creation into existence as an entity beyond himself. In Jesus, God wills to bear the consequences of his creation. To recognize Jesus as the Son of God is to recognize God accepting his responsibility for creation and leading creation back to himself from within it.

Because God is act and because all reality is act, the glory of God is found in God's action. The Hebrew root of the word *glory* is a word meaning "weight" or "riches." The glory of a person, accordingly, is the "weight" or "riches" or "worth" of the person. Even today we speak of a person's worth as the person's weight. We all know people who are "lightweights" and "heavyweights"; taken in that sense, a person's weight is the person's true nature and identity. A person's nature is the person's worth, and that is the person's glory. Influenced by their Jewish heritage, the first Christians saw God's glory — they experienced the presence of God, the "weight" or nature of God — dwelling among them in the life of Jesus. In Jesus, God made the action of his will, the spontaneity of his Spirit, available to human beings. God's glory was revealed on earth.

The scandal of Christianity was to find glory in the cross of Jesus Christ. The cross, an instrument of shame, became a sign of glory because through it the reality of God's love was proved. Thus Jesus said, after Judas left the supper in the Upper Room in order to betray him, "Now the Son of Man has been glorified, and God has been glorified in him" (John 13:31). We can understand how death on the cross is the glory of Christ when we understand that the weight (reality) of the cross and of the death Jesus suffered on the cross is the key to the reality (or the "weight") of Jesus' resurrection. The reality of the one who died is precisely the reality of the one who lives after death. The reality and the weight of Jesus' death are the reality and the glory of Jesus' resurrection. It is from the weight of Jesus' death and resurrection that the weight — or reality — of Christian hope arises in the world.

In Christian faith, reality arises from reality, action from action, life from life. That is why Paul writes to the Corinthians that "the kingdom of God depends not on talk but on power" (1 Cor. 4:20). Nothing in Christianity is theoretical; the only things Christians have are what God has actually given them. They make nothing up and try nothing by themselves for the first time. That is what it means to call Christianity a "historical religion." The historical nature of Christianity does not only refer to the general fact that it is one religion among many found in the world. Christians claim their religion to be historical in the stronger sense that everything truly Christian originates in a gift from God that has already been received and has already been tested in the ongoing life of the world. So it was that the crucifixion of Jesus tested the love of God — and the resurrection was God's answer to the test. Christianity begins in something that has already taken place and that is claimed to be going on today. People are called Christians when they allow, through the free act of their wills, the events of their lives to be incorporated into the events of the life of Jesus — events still going on because Jesus still lives.

The strength of Christian commitment in the world arises from the fact that the commitment originates within and out of the fabric of the world. Christian faith begins with the reality of the world, because it is the continuation of events that have already happened in the world. God's power and presence newly entered the world in Jesus, the man from Nazareth, the one so mysteriously filled with the Spirit of God that he was recognized to be the Christ. Christian belief arises from Jesus' life in the flesh, which is the reason that Christian faith is not out of place in the material world; Christian conviction arises out of the difference God's presence makes in the material world.

The strength of Christian belief is as real as the world because it arises from historical events in the world; that is why Christian faith is not afraid to confront the world and do battle in the world. But if the founding events claimed for Christianity did not actually happen, then Christianity is totally wrong, and there is no strength left to it at all. Historic events either happen or they do not; they are themselves or they are nothing. There is no middle ground. So there is no middle ground with Christianity:

either it is as real as the world or it is nothing. That is why Christianity cannot be reduced to talk; it is a religion of power, not words. The power of Christian faith is the presence of God — the Source of all reality — in our lives, and that presence can only be lived. To try to know God by hearing or by words is to miss God altogether, as Job, the Teacher of Ecclesiastes, and Paul testify.

Personal presence is more than anything we can say about it. Yet our common inclination is to try to evoke and equal the presence of God with verbal descriptions of it. But it simply cannot be done. If our descriptions were adequate to God's presence, God's presence would be reduced to our descriptions — and that would do nothing to help us solve our problems. What at first might appear to be a difficulty in our relating to God's presence may, in the end, be the only means of our getting beyond ourselves and recognizing the difference of God's presence from ours. Because human words cannot produce God's presence, the inadequacy of our words forces us beyond ourselves. To admit the difficulty we experience in talking about God's presence and our inability to make God's presence real for ourselves or for others by our words should not embarrass us. That admission is our liberation from ourselves. Recognizing our inability to talk about God adequately is the first step we must take in order to meet the only God who can be God.

Because God is a subject who can never be an object, God can only be spoken to, not about. Christian faith says that Jesus is truly God and truly human, meaning that the life of Jesus is the will of God expressed in human terms. As human, Jesus can be spoken about, for he had a bodily location in the world that can be described, as can his externally observed behavior; but, as God, the incarnate Son can only be spoken to. Love is always an activity directed toward another, and the only thing that will satisfy a lover is to be with the beloved. God so loves the world that he sends his Son into the world to be God-with-us in the world. As the Spirit-filled Son of God, Jesus is God-with-us in the world in such an intimate manner that we are always speaking to God simply by living the events of our lives. Through the flesh of the incarnate Word, God so immediately enters the events of our lives that we refuse to recognize the immediacy of his presence with us if we only talk to him *about* our lives. In Jesus, God is present with us more intimately than our words and prior to our words.

Jesus is God's placing himself not only in but within our situation so that God's presence is an ever-present resource from beyond us available to us in our lives. Because of God's presence with us in Jesus, a presence now universalized by the outpouring of the Spirit on the whole world at Pentecost, we are speaking to Jesus, and so to God, as we speak to, live with, and suffer with each other. With Jesus we are ourselves with God, and God is himself with us. God's intimacy with us and concern about us are more than we can fathom, because they are *gifts* of himself that God makes to us. Because the Word of God has been made flesh and still dwells among us in the Spirit, we talk to God when we talk to each other and even when we think to ourselves. God is the only place he can be in our lives as God — immediately present without any intermediary. If we will but recognize that presence, we will find, as Job did, that God's presence changes everything — but at a level of reality that escapes words and transports human expectation.

There is no doubt that Jesus was a healer. When John the Baptist sent two of his disciples to ask Jesus whether he was the one whose coming was awaited, Luke's Gospel tells us that "Jesus had just then cured many people of diseases, plagues, and evil spirits, and had given sight to many who were blind. And he answered them, 'Go and tell John what you have seen and heard: the blind receive their sight, the lame walk, the lepers are cleansed, the deaf hear, the dead are raised, the poor have good news brought to them'" (Luke 7:21-22). Such healing and liberation as Luke reports were signs long expected to herald the coming of the Messiah. Giving sight to the blind, enabling a mute to speak, curing a woman who suffered from hemorrhages, curing all manner of disease, and even restoring the dead to life — these are events that cannot be separated from both the proclamation and the person of Jesus.

It is the will of Jesus — who is the will of God — to heal and to restore and to liberate. Just to declare his will by word was sufficient to heal the servant of a centurion at Capernaum. The centurion had said to Jesus, "Lord, I am not worthy to have you come under my roof; but only speak the word, and my servant will be healed" (Matt. 8:8). Marveling at the centurion's faith, Jesus replied that it would be done according to the centurion's faith, and the servant was healed at the hour of Jesus' word. Just before the centurion came to Jesus, Jesus had healed a leper, and immediately following the healing of the servant, Jesus entered Peter's house and cured Peter's mother-in-law of a fever.

Again and again we read of Jesus having compassion on a crowd gathered about him and healing the sick who were presented to him (cf. Matt. 12:15; 14:14). The disciples healed in Jesus' name, as did Peter, who healed a man who had been lame from birth. He sat begging at a gate of the temple where his friends had placed him; Peter healed him "in the name of Jesus Christ of Nazareth" (Acts 3:6). The letter of James speaks of elders of the church healing the sick by praying for them and "anointing them with oil in the name of the Lord" (5:14). Paul also cured the sick by praying for them with the laying on of hands (Acts 28:8).

In some of the accounts of the crowd scenes in the New Testament, it is said that Jesus healed all who were brought to him. A large number of healings are recorded in the New Testament, so many that we must accept the fact that those who knew Jesus attributed many healings to him. Healings, as I mentioned, were one of the signs of the coming of the Messiah, and there had to be enough of them to show that a new age or epoch truly had arrived with the coming of Jesus. Matthew's Gospel reports that "Jesus went about all the cities and villages, teaching in their synagogues, and proclaiming the good news of the kingdom, and curing every disease and every sickness" (Matt. 9:35).

We can understand why Jesus was reported to have cured "every disease and every sickness," since that was critical to his being accepted as the Messiah, but understanding that connection does not mean that a great number of healings did not occur. But even granting the large number of healings attributed to Jesus, healings did not take place magically everywhere in the Messianic age that Jesus inaugurated. When Jesus returned to his hometown, we read that he did not do many "deeds of power" there because of the unbelief of his neighbors (Matt. 13:54-58). In one instance, the disciples were not able to cure an epileptic by their prayer, although Jesus effected the cure by his command (Matt. 17:14-18). Illness did not cease throughout the world, nor did cures occur widely enough for any other than the immediate disciples of Jesus to conclude that the Messianic age had begun with Jesus.

Even taking the New Testament witness to Jesus at face value does not remove all of the mystery surrounding faith healing. Enough narrative evidence and witness are offered to justify the belief that what is called spiritual healing can occur in the name of Jesus, but to admit that it can occur does not magically — or scientifically — assure that it will occur in a given instance. To believe that Jesus is the Spirit-filled Son of God is to believe that he came to heal the sick and that healing can occur today in his name, but the nature of such healing must still be seen, accepted, and understood from a perspective of reality that is God's alone — and that can never be ours.

Taking everything together that I have said in these pages, I believe I have shown the reasonableness of praying to God with the expectation that the sick can be both healed and cured. The issues we have discussed about the nature of human life, what it means to be a person, and our relation to God in our lives are issues that make a difference to more than just the healing of the sick. We have talked about the meaningfulness of life in general and about the nature and outcome of the struggle between good and evil in which human beings are involved in every dimension of their lives. We have discovered that internal spontaneity is the center and source of our lives as persons, and we have subsequently discovered that we depend upon the spontaneous act of will of a personal Source who is the Source of all sources. Our most immediate experience of ourselves convinces us of the meaningfulness of our lives, and of the whole universe, only within and from the spontaneous activity of a living God.

The general meaningfulness of life and of the universe reveals the presence of a providential goal for our lives and for the universe. We do not come from ourselves; we depend on a Source beyond us. We thus believe that the will of God can be seen in a general manner in the universe and in our lives. God creates the universe to be itself, but the universe cannot be itself by itself. Everything that exists depends upon the will of God; that we can say with certainty. But we cannot read the will of God with equal certainty in many of the specific events of our lives. We were not without problems at the beginning of our discussion, and we are not without problems now. We now, however, have a personal context for our problems that affords us a reasonable hope that human life has a value which exceeds its physical components and which cannot be destroyed by whatever happens in the world.

Throughout this discussion I have emphasized the difference between what are often referred to as "words" and "deeds." The phrase "words and deeds" domesticates a distinction whose real significance extends far beyond what we happen to say or do. A basic distinction of all reality is that between the activity of actually occurring events and the verbal patterns or concepts by which that activity is described. The ultimate reality of the universe is the interaction of forces whose dynamic activity we try to describe in the physical sciences. The point to recognize is that the activities which constitute the events making up the universe are more than the patterns of relations we abstract from them and use to describe them. The action of the universe and of our lives is to the verbal description of the universe and of our lives as fire is to paper. Act and action are the ultimate constituents of reality, and we have found the ultimate act and action to be the spontaneity of free will. Such activity is the only activity in our experience that can account for itself, and that capacity makes it the only activity that can account for all other activity.

History is a chain of events. History, as it occurs, is activity, and what does not actively occur is not historical. In Jesus Christ, Christians see God actively identifying himself with the activity constituting the basic reality of the world. That means God enters the world historically — God enters the world in Jesus with the same reality as the world. God enters the world in an event so that he can be with us and be available to us in the events of our lives. We cannot have conceptual clarity about what God is doing, nor should we be expected to have it, as I have tried to show. But because God universalized the life of Jesus in the world through the outpouring of the Spirit of Jesus upon the world, God's presence is so immediately with us in the events of our lives that the meaning of the events — and our ability to survive the events — is transformed in the never-failing action of that presence. God's presence, the Source of all, changes all. In God's presence, a disease may be cured; that is one difference God's presence may make. But, whether a cure occurs or not, recognizing God's presence makes a total difference in a situation; it makes a difference that is healing and liberating. Such a difference, brought by the infinitude of God's presence, cannot be captured in our words, but its transforming power arises from that very fact. Ask Job!

Praying or talking to God is not only a reasonable thing for us to do; it is the only thing we can do. We cannot properly talk about God, as I have tried to show, but, even more important than that, God has freely willed us into existence just so that we will freely will ourselves back to him. In the life of Jesus Christ, God has identified himself with us and with our world, and in the universalized presence of Jesus in the world through the outpouring of the Spirit of the Christ at Pentecost, God has identified his immediate presence in the world with everything we suffer — and with everything we do to each other — in the world. We are with God "in Christ," as Paul puts it; and all of our prayer to God is "through Jesus Christ our Lord," as the church puts it. As Emmanuel, Jesus is "God with us" (Matt. 1:23), and we are with God when we live with Jesus in the Spirit.

The life of Jesus is meant to be our life, and it can be if we will Jesus' will. Such mutual willing is how the spontaneity of our lives is incorporated into the spontaneity of Jesus' life. In the beginning of our discussion, I talked about the flow and spontaneity of our lives, and I said that flow can be described as a rhythm. Hans Urs von Balthasar has suggested that the unwavering spontaneity of Jesus' life is the decisive feature of his life, and von Balthasar has gone on to say that, in the Christian life, the rhythm of Christ's spontaneous self-giving becomes the believer's own.

The Word of God is a person, and the spontaneity of fully personal living prevents our ever reducing the Word of God to a static plan or system of concepts. Living in the Spirit of the Messiah, Christians do not conceive a plan or final state of human life that they try to bring about; they do not live by goals they conceive. Rather, they live in the presence of One who calls them beyond themselves into the active spontaneity of his love. Self-lessness rather than self-fulfillment describes the action of Christian living. The "goal" of Christians is something they discover, something given to them beyond their intentions, rather than something they conceive and bring about.

Christians live by being taken into Christ's life; they do not live from benefits that Christ's life won for them. To try to live from benefits believed to be won by Christ for others is to try to relate to Christ externally; it is to relate to him as an object. To try to live from the benefits of Jesus' life is to attempt to reduce Jesus to no more than the means of getting what we want. That is hardly "dying to self" and finding "new life" in him.

The Christian life is incorporation into an action: the action of Jesus' life becomes the action of our lives. For a Christian, salvation is not a privilege he or she can receive; it is an activity into which he or she is taken. The death (and resurrection) of Jesus is often called a vicarious sacrifice made for others, but in no way was Jesus, as a vicarious sacrifice, substituted for others so that they could remain themselves. That is why Paul, in his letter to the Galatians, told them that in their baptism they had "put on Christ"; from that time on they were "of Christ," no longer living in themselves for themselves (Gal. 3:26-29). When our inner lives are thus changed, we become "strong in the Lord and in the strength of his power" (Eph. 6:10).

The offering of a gift to someone is of unique significance. The giving of a gift is the way one person chooses another for who he or she is without external constraint or necessity. We feel liberated to be most fully ourselves when we receive a gift, because a true gift is given to us for no other reason than for who we are. A gift is the spontaneous recognition by one person of the spontaneity of another person. The greatest gift we can offer another is ourselves; that is the gift of love.

Christians see the life of Jesus to be God's gift of himself to us. In Jesus, God so offers himself to us that the dependent spontaneity of our lives is sustained everlastingly by the self-sufficient spontaneity of God's own life. God is the Person *in whom* we become persons; God is not the *means* by which we become persons. We become ourselves in God, by giving ourselves up to God. We do not become ourselves by trying to use God for ourselves.

To accept God's gift of himself to us is freely to will his will for us; our freely willing God's free will for us is our true life. In that life, we are at once ultimately spontaneous and ultimately secure — no matter what happens to us in the world.